MILLET REVOLUTION

THE ANCIENT SECRET TO MODERN WELLNESS

Parimala Jaggesh & Gururaj Jaggesh

INDIA • SINGAPORE • MALAYSIA

ISBN
Paperback 979-8-89744-654-4
Hardcase 979-8-89906-271-1

DEDICATION

"To the brothers and sisters who toil under the sun and rain to nourish us.

This book is a tribute to you.

"Farmers, the true heroes of our land"

#Gratitude #Farmers #MilletRevolution"

"This journey began with a blessing — a powerful moment with Hon'ble Prime Minister Shri Narendra Modi ji, who inspired me to carry forward the mission of millets for India's wellness."

CONTENTS

HOW THIS BOOK WAS BORN - A PARADIGM SHIFT

There are moments in life that shift the very course of our journey. One such moment happened in March 2023, when I had the honour of meeting our country's esteemed Prime Minister Shri.Narendra Modi Ji.

Visionaries have a way of looking at life differently from the rest of us.

As we passionately discussed about health and wellness from our kitchens using our ancient traditional wisdom, he saw something beyond my words. He saw a purpose.

Then, in that unforgettable moment, he entrusted me with a mission:

"Take it upon your shoulders to simplify the addition of millets into people's lives."

That statement wasn't just a suggestion. It was a call to action. A challenge. A responsibility. A validation of the path I had chosen.

That day changed me. It gave me a renewed sense of purpose. I realised that my work was no longer just about individual consultations. It had to go beyond that.

It had to become a REVOLUTION

"Millets are not just food; they are a legacy—a gift from our ancestors that holds the power to transform health for generations to come. By bringing them back to our kitchens, we are not just reviving an ancient grain; we are reviving a healthier future."

"One simple change—adding millets to ONE of our daily meals—can break the cycle of lifestyle diseases, nourish our families, and redefine the way we approach health. This is not just a diet shift; it is a generational transformation."

This book is a small attempt to serve the world—with love, with healing, and with the wisdom of our ancestors.

It is not just about food; it is a journey of transformation, of going back to our roots, and of offering something meaningful to every home."

It's about healing, harmony, and seva through every grain."

And so, this book was born.

OFFICE OF GURUDEV SRI SRI RAVI SHANKAR
ART OF LIVING INTERNATIONAL CENTRE, 21 KM KANAKAPURA ROAD,
UDAYPURA, BANGALORE - 82, INDIA P | +91.80.67262616 F | +91.80.28432833
SECRETARIAT@ARTOFLIVING.ORG | WWW.SRISRI.ORG | WWW.ARTOFLIVING.ORG

April 2, 2025

MESSAGE

Nature has abundantly blessed this land with the gift of millets, a powerhouse of strength, vitality, and well-being.

For generations, these ancient grains have nourished life, growing easily with minimal water and care. Yet, in recent decades, they have slowly vanished from our daily diets, replaced by lesser alternatives.

The Millet Revolution: The Ancient Secret to Modern Wellness is a commendable effort to bring millets back to our plates.

May this book awaken a deeper reverence for food, the body, and Mother Earth. When we honour these, we create a healthier and happier world for all.

Loka Samasta Sukhino Bhavantu!

Blessings and Best wishes
-Gurudev Sri Sri Ravi Shankar

"Tasty, Healthy, Simple"

"Scan for Nutritious Yet Delicious Recipes."

"**The Shree Anna Conference** lit a spark within me—transforming my passion for millets into a mission to heal and nourish the world."

INTRODUCTION

The Millet Movement Back to the Future with Millets: Rediscovering Ancient Grains for Modern Living.

Hello there, and welcome to a journey that is both ancient and refreshingly modern!

I'm Parimala Jaggesh, the founder of Alamirap Nutrition, and just like you, I once found myself overwhelmed by the endless choices in the world of healthy eating. The market is flooded with exotic superfoods and complicated diet plans, but I've always believed that the most powerful solutions are often the simplest. That's how I rediscovered the magic of millets – our ancient grains for modern health.

My Journey with Millets.

My journey with millets began many years ago when I was diagnosed with type-2 diabetes. The struggle was real – from balancing my blood sugar levels to finding foods that were both tasty and healthy. After trying several diets, I stumbled upon an ancient wisdom that was right in front of me all along – millets. I started experimenting with millets in my kitchen, combining traditional recipes with modern cooking techniques. To my surprise, not only did my blood sugar stabilise, but I also felt more energetic and healthier. This wasn't just my experience.

As I introduced millets to my clients at Alamirap Nutrition, I witnessed hundreds of lives transforming – people losing weight, managing diabetes, balancing hormones, and living healthier lives.

This book is born from those experiences, from the countless kitchen experiments, and from the heartfelt testimonies of my clients. It's my way of sharing with you the joy and magic of cooking with millets.

Why Millets Matter?

Millets are not just grains; they are tiny powerhouses of nutrition. For thousands of years, they were the staple food in many parts of the world, especially in India. But as polished rice and refined wheat took over, millets were pushed to the background. Packed with fibre, protein, vitamins, and minerals, millets are incredibly nutritious and versatile. They help regulate blood sugar, boost immunity, improve digestion, and even aid in Weight Management.

Not just that, they are gluten-free and suitable for people with dietary restrictions. If you're someone who believes in the age-old saying, "Let food be thy medicine and medicine be thy food," then millets are your perfect companions.

What to Expect from This Book

This is not just another recipe book. It's a guide to a healthier lifestyle, a collection of memories, and a testament to the power of simplicity in nutrition. Whether you are a beginner curious about millets or a seasoned cook looking for new ideas, this book has something for everyone.

- Easy-to-Follow Recipes: From breakfast to dinner, snacks to desserts – this book covers it all, with step-by-step instructions that make cooking fun and easy.
- Nutritional Insights: Learn not just how to cook but also why to cook with millets. Understand the health benefits and how each recipe contributes to your well-being.
- Cultural Stories and Fun Facts: Rediscover the cultural heritage of millets, their traditional uses, and fun facts that connect you to your roots.

- Quick Access with Technology: Love the feel of a book but also enjoy the ease of technology? Simply scan the QR codes for video demonstrations.

How to Use This Book?

This book is designed to be your kitchen companion, your guide to a healthier lifestyle.

Here's how you can make the most of it:

- Explore the Chapters: Each chapter is dedicated to a specific health benefit or category, making it easier to find what you need.
- Mix and Match: Millets are incredibly versatile. Feel free to experiment and mix recipes across chapters. Plan Your Meals: Use the suggested meal planners to create balanced and nutritious meals for yourself and your family.
- Share and Inspire: Don't keep the goodness to yourself. Share your creations on social media, tag Alamirap Nutrition, and inspire others to join the Millet Movement.

A Note from My Heart

Since decades, I have seen too many people suffer—struggling with health issues that could have been prevented, trapped in cycles of medication, frustration, and despair. And I cannot stay silent.

This book is more than just recipes; it is my mission, my purpose, my life's work. I want to help you break free from the burden of poor health, to show you that the right food can heal, energise, and transform your life. Millets are not just an ingredient—they are a path to strength, balance, and lasting wellness.

I have poured my heart into these pages. You deserve to feel your best. You deserve a vibrant, healthy life. Let this book be your guide. Now is the time for change.

Chapter 1

MILLET BASICS:

The NINE SUPERSTARS – Get to Know Your Millets:

Welcome to the world of millets!

If you're new to these tiny powerhouses of nutrition, don't worry – you're about to be pleasantly surprised. And if you've already heard about them but never got around to trying them, this chapter will give you the perfect start.

Millets are not just another health fad. They are ancient grains that have been nourishing humanity for over 10,000 years. Yes, you read that right! These humble grains were once the staple food for many civilisations across Asia and Africa.

In this book, we will be exploring "The Nine Superstars of Millets."

Let's get to know the nine varieties of millets that will soon become your kitchen favourites:

1. Sorghum (Jowar) – Rich in iron and protein, great for boosting energy.
2. Pearl Millet (Bajra) – High in fibre, ideal for heart health and diabetes management.
3. Foxtail Millet (Navane) – High in protein and iron, great for muscle health.
4. Finger Millet (Ragi) – Calcium-rich, perfect for bone health.
5. Proso Millet (Baragu) – High in protein and lecithin, supports brain health.
6. Kodo Millet (Harka) – Rich in antioxidants, aids in detoxification.
7. Barnyard Millet (Oodalu) – Low in calories, perfect for weight watchers.
8. Little Millet (Saame) – Low glycaemic index, suitable for Weight Management and diabetes.
9. Browntop Millet (Korale) – Full of minerals, excellent for immunity and digestion.

Basics of Cooking with Millets

Cooking with millets is simple, nourishing, and incredibly rewarding. If you've never cooked with millets before, don't worry—let's explore how to start today!

1. Choosing the Right Millet
   Each type of millet has a unique texture and taste. Here's a quick guide:
   - Foxtail Millet – Light, fluffy, great for pulao and upma.
   - Barnyard Millet – Fast-cooking, perfect for khichdi and porridge.
   - Little Millet – Soft, good for idlis, dosas, and rice substitutes.
   - Kodo Millet – Nutty and filling, works well in salads and pulao.
   - Bajra (Pearl Millet) & Jowar (Sorghum) – Hearty and dense, ideal for rotis and porridges.
   - Ragi (Finger Millet) – Rich in calcium, best for porridges, dosas, and rotis.
2. Preparing Millets for Cooking
   - Rinse Well – Wash millets 2-3 times under running water to remove dust and excess starch.
   - Soaking (Optional, but Recommended) – Soak for 4-6 hours (or overnight) to improve digestion and reduce cooking time.
   - Roasting (For Certain Dishes) – Dry roast millets before cooking for a nutty flavour and better texture.
3. Cooking Millets – The Right Water Ratio
   Millets cook differently from rice. Here's a general guide:
   - For Fluffy Texture (Like Rice) – Use 1:2 millet-to-water ratio.
   - For Soft & Sticky Texture (Like Porridge) – Use 1:3 or 1:4 ratio.
   - For Flour-Based Recipes (Roti, Dosa, Idli) – Use millets in ground form or mix with other flours.
4. **Cooking Methods**
   - Stovetop Method – Bring water to a boil, add millets, cover, and cook on low heat for 10-15 minutes.
   - Pressure Cooker – Use a 1:2.5 ratio, cook for 2 whistles, then let steam release naturally.

- Instant Pot – Set to 'Pressure Cook' for 5-6 minutes with a 1:2 water ratio.
- Steaming – Ideal for idlis, dhoklas, and dumplings using millet flour.

5. Using Millets in Everyday Meals
   - Replace white rice with cooked millets in curries, pulao, or biryanis.
   - Use millet flour for rotis, pancakes, and baked goods.
   - Make dosa and idli batter using fermented millet.
   - Prepare warm porridges for a nutritious breakfast.
   - Add millets to soups, salads, and even desserts like kheer or payasam.
6. Experiment and Enjoy!

   If you've never cooked with millets before, start simple. Cook a small batch, taste it, and try swapping it into familiar dishes. The more you experiment, the more comfortable you'll become.

Millets are versatile, delicious, and life-changing. Let's start cooking today!

A Fun Fact to Inspire You.

Did you know?

Millets are the original superfoods, and they've been mentioned in ancient texts like the Yajur Veda, dating back to 4500 BC!

Coming up next, we'll dive deeper into detailed recipes starting from preparation tips to serving suggestions, get ready to cook up a storm with millets as your star ingredient. But for now, give yourself a pat on the back – you're on the path to healthier cooking,

"One millet meal at a time."

Translations of Millets in Different Languages

Millet Type English	Kannada ಕನ್ನಡ	Telugu (తెలుగు)	Tamil (தமிழ்)	Malayalam (മലയാളം)	Hindi (हिंदी)
Pearl	ಸಜ್ಜೆ	సజ్జలు	கம்பு	കമ്പം	बाजरा
Foxtail	ನಾವಣೆ	కొర్రలు	தினை	തിന	कंगनी
Finger	ರಾಗಿ	రాగి	கேழ்வரகு	റാഗി	मडुआ
Barnyard	ಊದಲು	ఊదలు	குடைவளை	കുതിരവാലി	सांवा
Little	ಸಾಮೆ	సామలు	சாமை	ചാമ	कुटकी
Kodo	ಹಾರಕ	అరికెలు	வரகு	അവരക്	कोदो
Proso	ಬರಗು	వరిగలు	பனிவரகு	പനി വരക്	चेना
Sorghum	ಜೋಳ	జొన్నలు	சொளம்	ചൊല്ല	ज्वार
Browntop	ಹುಚ್ಚು ನಾವಣೆ	అండకొర్ర	புல்நவணை	പുള്കര	ब्राउनटॉप बाजरा

Chapter 2

WEIGHT MANAGEMENT

"Lose the Weight, Keep the Taste: Millets to the Rescue!"

"Take care of your body. It's the only place you have to live." – Jim Rohn

Welcome to the Weight Management chapter where we explore how millets can be your secret weapon for shedding extra weight and powering an active lifestyle. If you have been searching for a natural, wholesome way to boost your fitness journey, millets might just be the game-changer you need.

This chapter is all about practicality and sustainability—helping you embrace millets in an easy, delicious, and results-driven way. We'll cover:

- ✓ Why millets are excellent for weight management
- ✓ Meal plans and fitness-friendly recipes
- ✓ Pre-and post-workout millet meals
- ✓ Motivation, success stories, and tips

So, let's dive in and discover how these ancient grains can supercharge your modern health journey—in a fun, sustainable way!

Why Millets Are Great for Weight Management & Fitness

Millets aren't called "super grains" for nothing. When it comes to weight management and fitness, they check all the right boxes.

1. High Fiber = Full Tummy, Fewer Cravings
    - ✓ Millets are packed with dietary fiber, keeping you fuller for longer.
    - ✓ Helps curb cravings and prevent overeating.
    - ✓ Supports healthy digestion, reducing bloating.
    - ✓ Say goodbye to mid-morning hunger pangs and junk food temptations!
2. Complex Carbs for Steady Energy
    - ✓ Unlike refined grains that cause energy crashes, millets release energy slowly.
    - ✓ Low to medium glycemic index = less insulin spikes (which means less fat storage!).
    - ✓ Perfect for workouts—gives you stamina without feeling drained.

3. Rich in Essential Nutrients
    - ✓ High in B-vitamins = better metabolism & fat burning.
    - ✓ Magnesium & phosphorus aid muscle recovery and energy production.
    - ✓ Iron prevents fatigue, calcium strengthens bones.
4. Plant Protein Power
    - ✓ Millets contain good-quality protein—important for muscle repair & fat loss.
    - ✓ Ragi (finger millet) & foxtail millet are particularly protein-rich.
    - ✓ When combined with lentils, beans, or dairy, millets provide all essential amino acids.
5. Naturally Gluten-Free & Easy to Digest
    - ✓ Helps those who feel bloated or sluggish after eating wheat.
    - ✓ Supports gut health, which is key to weight management.
    - ✓ Reduces inflammation and improves nutrient absorption.
6. Versatile, Delicious & Never Boring!
    - ✓ From fluffy porridge to crispy snacks, savoury upma to indulgent desserts—millets can do it all!
    - ✓ You'll never feel deprived, making healthy eating enjoyable & sustainable.

In summary, millets help you lose weight the right way—keeping you full, energized, and nourished. Now, let's get practical with some millet-powered meal plans and fitness recipes!

"A goal without a plan is just a wish."

No matter who you are—a busy mom, a determined athlete, a student juggling studies, or a corporate professional with a packed schedule—millets can fit right into your lifestyle.

Don't worry, we've got you covered!

Here's a simple, flexible one-day meal plan to help you get started on your Millet-Powered Meal Plans for Active Lifestyles

Recipe 1 – "Ragi -Banana Rockstar Smoothie: Bliss in Every Sip!"

(Serves 2) - Breakfast

This creamy, nutrient-packed Ragi-Banana Smoothie is perfect for breakfast or a post-workout snack! It's rich in fibre, protein, and essential minerals, keeping you energised and full for longer.

Ingredients:

- Ragi flour (Finger Millet Flour) – 2 tbsp
- Ripe banana – 1 large (or 2 small)
- Milk (or plant-based milk) – 1.5 cups
- Yogurt (optional for extra creaminess) – ¼ cup
- Honey or Dates – 1 tbsp (adjust to taste)
- Chia seeds or Flaxseeds – 1 tsp (optional, for added nutrition)
- Cinnamon powder – ¼ tsp (for flavour)
- Cocoa powder – 1 tsp (optional, for a chocolatey twist)
- Ice cubes – 4-5

Step-by-Step Directions:

1. Cook the Ragi Flour
    - In a small pan, mix 2 tbsp ragi flour with ½ cup water and stir continuously on low heat.
    - Cook for 3-4 minutes until it forms a thick, smooth paste.
    - Let it cool completely before using in the smoothie.
2. Blend Everything Together
    - In a blender, add the cooled ragi paste, banana, milk, yogurt (if using), honey/dates, chia seeds/flaxseeds, cinnamon powder, and cocoa powder (if adding).
    - Blend until smooth and creamy.

3. **Adjust Consistency**
   - If it's too thick, add a little more milk or water.
   - If you like it colder, add a few more ice cubes and blend again.
4. Serve & Enjoy!
   - Pour into a glass or bowl, garnish with banana slices, nuts, or seeds, and enjoy your delicious, energy-boosting Ragi-Banana Smoothie!

Pari's Super Tips:

✓ For extra protein, add a scoop of protein powder or a spoonful of peanut butter.

✓ For a nutty flavour, use almond or coconut milk instead of regular milk.

✓ For a thicker smoothie bowl, reduce the liquid and top with granola, nuts, or fresh fruits.

Enjoy your wholesome, power-packed smoothie!

Variations of the ABOVE:

First cook ragi as explained above and experiment with these combinations

1. Ragi-Spinach Energizer (Ragi, spinach, banana, and almond milk)
   The banana balances the earthy taste of spinach, making it a delicious and nutritious.
2. Ragi-Papaya Gut Booster (Ragi, papaya, and yogurt)
   Papaya aids digestion and pairs well with ragi for a creamy, gut-friendly smoothie.
3. Ragi-Cucumber Refresh (Ragi, cucumber, and mint)
   A cooling, hydrating smoothie perfect for hot days and post-workout recovery.
4. Ragi-Pomegranate Glow (Ragi, pomegranate, and coconut water)
   Rich in antioxidants, this smoothie supports glowing skin and overall wellness.
5. Ragi-Tomato Detox (Ragi, tomato, and ginger)
   A tangy and spicy twist, packed with vitamin C and detoxifying properties!

Recipe 2 – Crunchy Jowar/Sorghum Puffs (Serves 2) – Guilt-free Snacking

A light, crispy, and protein-rich snack, Crunchy Jowar Puffs are perfect for guilt-free munching. They're high in fibre, gluten-free, and packed with energy—ideal for tea-time or an on-the-go snack.

Ingredients:

- Jowar (Sorghum) grains – ½ cup
- Ghee or Coconut Oil – 1 tsp
- Turmeric Powder – ¼ tsp
- Chilli Powder or Black Pepper – ½ tsp (adjust to taste)
- Salt – ¼ tsp
- Chaat Masala (Optional, for extra flavour) – ¼ tsp

Step-by-Step Directions:

1. Pop the Jowar
    - Heat a heavy-bottomed pan on medium heat.
    - Once hot, add a few jowar grains to test—if they start popping, the pan is ready.
    - Add the rest of the jowar and keep stirring continuously to prevent burning.
    - The grains will start popping within 3-4 minutes. Keep stirring until most are puffed.
    - Remove from heat and let them cool slightly.
2. Flavour the Puffs
    - In a separate small pan, heat ghee or coconut oil on low flame.
    - Add turmeric, chilli powder, and salt, stirring for a few seconds.
    - Immediately pour this over the popped jowar and toss well to coat.
    - Final Touch & Serve - Sprinkle chaat masala
    - Let them cool completely before storing in an airtight container.
    - Enjoy as a crispy, healthy snack anytime!

Recipe 3 – LUNCH - Millet Buddha Bowl – Veg & Non-Veg Versions (Serves 2)

A Millet Buddha Bowl is a balanced, wholesome meal packed with fibre, protein, and essential nutrients. This bowl combines millets, fresh veggies, proteins, and a flavourful dressing for a nourishing and delicious meal. Below are both vegetarian and non-vegetarian versions so you can choose what works best for you!

Vegetarian/Nonvegetarian Millet Buddha Bowl

You can just flip the Protein choices and create your own Magical Buddha Bowl

Ingredients:

Base (Grain)

- Cooked Millet (Foxtail, Barnyard, or Little Millet) – 1 cup

Vegetable Toppings

- Carrot (Julienned) – ¼ cup
- Cucumber (Sliced) – ¼ cup
- Cherry Tomatoes (Halved) – ¼ cup
- Steamed Broccoli – ¼ cup
- Avocado (Sliced or Mashed, Optional) – ½ piece

Protein

Vegetarian Options

- Chickpeas (Boiled or Roasted) – ½ cup
- Tofu (Grilled or Pan-Seared) – ½ cup, cubed

Non-vegetarian Options

- Grilled Chicken (Sliced) – ½ cup OR
- Boiled Egg (Sliced) – 1 large OR
- Grilled Prawns (Optional, for seafood lovers) – ½ cup

Dressing

- Olive Oil – 1 tbsp
- Lemon Juice – 1 tbsp
- Tahini or Yogurt – 1 tbsp
- Garlic (Minced) – 1 clove
- Salt & Pepper – To taste
- Honey (Optional, for sweetness) – ½ tsp

Toppings (Optional)

- Crushed Nuts (Almonds, Cashews, or Peanuts) – 1 tbsp
- Feta Cheese (Optional, for extra flavour) – 1 tbsp

Step-by-Step Directions

1. Cook the Millet
   - Rinse ½ cup millet and cook with 1 cup water until soft and fluffy. Let it cool.
2. Prepare the Protein
   - For Veg: Roast chickpeas or pan-sear tofu with a little olive oil and salt.
   - For Non-Veg: Grill chicken, boil an egg, or cook prawns with light seasoning.
3. Chop & Prep the Vegetables
   - Julienne, slice, or dice all the veggies as per preference.
4. Mix the Dressing
   - In a bowl, whisk all the dressing ingredients until smooth.
5. Assemble the Buddha Bowl
   - Place the cooked millet as the base.
   - Arrange the veggies and protein beautifully on top.
   - Drizzle the dressing generously over the bowl.
   - Garnish with nuts, seeds, or herbs of your choice.
6. Serve & Enjoy!
   - Mix everything before eating or enjoy each section separately!

Pari's Super Tip

For an extra crunch, roast chickpeas or nuts before adding them to your Buddha bowl. This adds texture and enhances flavour!

Enjoy your Millet Buddha Bowl—nutritious, satisfying, and full of goodness!

Recipe 4 – Dinner: Dreamy Kodo Millet "Fried Rice" with Tofu/Chicken (Serves 2)

This Kodo Millet Fried Rice is packed with protein, fibre, and calming nutrients to support a good night's sleep. Kodo millet is light on digestion, and tofu provides plant-based protein, making this dish perfect for a soothing yet fulfilling dinner.

Ingredients:

Base (Millet & Protein)

- Kodo Millet – ½ cup (cooked in 1 cup water)
- Tofu (Firm, Cubed) – ½ cup / Chicken cooked and shredded ½ cup
- Sesame Oil or Ghee – 1 tbsp

Vegetables (Choose any)

- Carrot (Diced) – ¼ cup
- Bell Peppers (Chopped) – ¼ cup
- Green Beans (Chopped) – ¼ cup
- Spring Onion (Chopped, for garnish) – 2 tbsp

Sleep-Boosting Flavours & Seasoning

- Garlic (Minced, promotes relaxation) – 2 cloves
- Ginger (Grated, aids digestion) – 1 tsp
- Soy Sauce (or Tamari, for umami flavour) – 1 tbsp
- Turmeric Powder (Anti-inflammatory, optional) – ¼ tsp
- Black Pepper (Boosts absorption) – ½ tsp
- Salt – To taste

Toppings (Optional, for extra sleep benefits!)

- Pumpkin Seeds (Rich in magnesium, promotes relaxation) – 1 tbsp
- Sesame Seeds (Adds crunch & calcium for sleep support) – 1 tsp

Step-by-Step Directions:

1. Cook the Millet
   - Rinse ½ cup Kodo millet and cook it in 1 cup water until fluffy. Let it cool slightly.
2. Crisp the Tofu
   - Heat ½ tbsp sesame oil in a pan.
   - Add cubed tofu, sprinkle a little salt & black pepper, and sauté until golden brown on all sides (4-5 minutes).
   - Remove and set aside.
3. Sauté the Aromatics & Veggies
   - In the same pan, add remaining sesame oil and sauté garlic & ginger until fragrant.
   - Add chopped carrots, bell peppers, and green beans. Stir-fry for 2-3 minutes until slightly tender but still crisp.
4. Combine Everything
   - Add cooked millet, tofu, soy sauce, turmeric, and black pepper. Stir-fry for 2 minutes to blend the flavours.
5. Garnish & Serve
   - Sprinkle with pumpkin & sesame seeds for extra crunch and sleep-supporting nutrients.
   - Garnish with spring onions and serve warm!

Pari's Super Tip 🏆

For a deeper, comforting flavour, add a splash of warm almond or coconut milk at the end—this adds creaminess and extra relaxation benefits!

Enjoy your Dreamy Kodo Millet Fried Rice—delicious, nutritious, and perfect for a peaceful night's sleep!

SUCCESS STORY – 1

Revathy's Journey: From Exhaustion to Empowerment with Millets

Revathy sat on the park bench, rocking her six-month-old daughter in her arms. She loved her child more than anything, but motherhood had drained her.

She had always been an energetic woman, juggling work, family, and her passions. But after pregnancy, everything changed. Her body felt weak, her energy levels were gone, and every day was a struggle.

"I thought things would get better after delivery," she often told herself. But instead, she woke up every morning feeling more exhausted than the night before.

Her hair was falling out in clumps, her skin had lost its glow, and no matter what she ate, she felt bloated and sluggish. Sleep was broken, and worst of all, she didn't even recognize herself in the mirror anymore.

A Skeptic Meets a Solution

One afternoon, at a family gathering, Revathy's cousin casually mentioned my name.

"You should meet her," her cousin said. *"She changed the way I eat, and trust me, I've never felt better!"*

Revathy wasn't convinced.

"Millets? Those are for old people," she laughed. *"I need real food, not bird food."*

She had tried everything—protein powders, energy drinks, even the so-called "superfoods" from the internet—but nothing worked.

Still, after weeks of hesitation, she reached out. And that conversation changed everything.

The Turning Point

When I met Revathy, she was at her lowest.

"I don't have time for elaborate diets. I need something that works, something simple!" she told me, frustration in her voice.

"Then let's not make it complicated," I said. *"Let's start small."*

We didn't talk about cutting food but rather about adding the right food.

Instead of heavy breakfasts that made her feel sluggish, I suggested a warm, nourishing ragi porridge—a meal her grandmother had once made but she had long forgotten.

Instead of quick-fix sugary snacks, I gave her a recipe for millet energy balls that she could grab between feedings.

And most importantly, instead of focusing on weight loss, we focused on strength.

Small Steps, Big Changes

At first, Revathy didn't believe it. But within a week, she started noticing small changes. The afternoon crashes disappeared. The bloated feeling reduced.

Her mood lifted and for the first time in months, she felt strong.

With every passing day, she started exploring more. A Bajra roti instead of regular chapati. A foxtail millet pulao instead of white rice.

The best part? She never felt deprived.

As weeks turned into months, her hair grew thicker, her sleep improved, and she could carry her baby for hours without feeling exhausted.

One evening, after months of feeling lost, she stood in front of the mirror.

For the first time, she recognized herself again.

Not just as a mother, but as Revathy—the strong, confident woman she once was.

My Little Angel

Chapter 3

WORKOUTS AND MILLETS

Fuel, Perform, Recover: The Power of Millets for Workouts

When it comes to fitness, the right fuel and recovery can make all the difference. Whether you're lifting weights, running marathons, or simply staying active, what you eat before and after exercise directly impacts your performance and recovery.

Many people focus only on protein shakes and supplements, but the truth is, real food can provide all the essential nutrients your body needs—and millets are a powerhouse in this game!

The Workout Nutrition Formula: Timing is Everything!

1. The Pre-Workout Window (30-90 minutes before exercise)
    - This is your fueling phase—your body needs the right carbs, proteins, and hydration to sustain energy, improve endurance, and avoid fatigue.
2. Why is Pre-Workout Nutrition Important?
    - Boosts Energy – Fuels muscles for sustained performance.
    - Prevents Muscle Breakdown – Provides amino acids for strength.
    - Optimises Performance – Enhances stamina and endurance.
3. Best Pre-Workout Nutrients:
    - Complex Carbohydrates (for slow-release energy)
    - Moderate Protein (for muscle priming)
    - Hydration & Electrolytes (to prevent cramps & fatigue)
4. What Happens If You Skip It?
    - Low energy levels, early fatigue, and reduced strength.
    - Increased risk of muscle breakdown and injury.
5. Best Millets for Pre-Workout:
    - Foxtail Millet (Rich in B vitamins & slow-digesting carbs for endurance)
    - Little Millet (Easy to digest, prevents bloating before exercise)
    - Ragi (Finger Millet) (High in calcium & iron for bone strength and oxygen supply)

Recipe 5 – Bajra Power Bites: Energy Bombs for Your Workout

"Food is fuel. Eat to energize, not to crash."

Recipe Servings: 2 (Makes about 6 small energy balls)

Ingredients:

Base (Millet & Binders)

- Bajra (Pearl Millet) Flour – ¼ cup
- Rolled Oats (Optional, for texture) – 2 tbsp
- Peanut Butter or Almond Butter – 2 tbsp

Sweeteners & Energy Boosters

- Dates (Pitted and Chopped) – 4-5
- Honey or Jaggery Syrup – 1 tbsp

Nutrient Boosters

- Flaxseeds or Chia Seeds (For Omega-3 & Fiber) – 1 tsp
- Almonds or Cashews (Finely Chopped or Crushed) – 2 tbsp
- Cocoa Powder (Optional, for a chocolatey taste) – 1 tsp
- Cardamom Powder (For Flavor & Digestion Boost) – ¼ tsp

Binding Agent

- Ghee or Coconut Oil – 1 tsp

Step-by-Step Directions:

1. Dry Roast the Bajra Flour
   - Heat a pan on low-medium heat and dry roast ¼ cup bajra flour for about 3-4 minutes until it gives off a nutty aroma. Transfer to a bowl and let it cool.
2. Prepare the Sweetener Mix
   - In a small saucepan, heat 1 tbsp honey or jaggery syrup with 1 tsp ghee or coconut oil for about 30 seconds until slightly melted. Remove from heat and set aside.
3. Blend the Sticky Base
   - In a blender, pulse dates, peanut butter, and the sweetener mix until it forms a sticky paste. Add the flaxseeds or chia seeds and pulse again.
4. Mix Everything Together
   - In a mixing bowl, combine the roasted bajra flour, chopped nuts, cocoa powder, cardamom powder, and the blended date mixture.
   - Knead well until the mixture forms a dough-like consistency. If too dry, add 1 tsp warm water to adjust.
5. Shape the Energy Balls
   - Take small portions and roll them into bite-sized balls.
   - Coat with crushed nuts, sesame seeds, or desiccated coconut for extra crunch (optional).
6. Set & Store
   - Let the energy balls rest for 15 minutes to firm up.
   - Store in an airtight container and consume within 4-5 days.

Why These Bajra Energy Balls Work for Pre-Workout?

✓ Slow-releasing energy from bajra keeps you fueled for longer.

✓ Dates and jaggery provide natural sugars for an instant energy boost.

✓ Healthy fats from nuts and seeds enhance stamina.

✓ Protein from peanut butter and flaxseeds supports muscle priming.

Recipe 6 – "Mighty Jowar and Egg - Power Pancakes"

Fuel Up, Go Strong!

Why This Pancake is Perfect for Pre-Workout

☑ Slow-Releasing Carbs from Millets – Prevents mid-workout fatigue.

☑ High-Quality Protein from Eggs – Supports muscle activation and endurance.

☑ Healthy Fats for Sustained Fuel – Keeps you full without bloating.

☑ Electrolytes & Minerals – Prevent muscle cramps and dehydration.

☑ Anti-Inflammatory Spices – Reduces muscle soreness post-workout.

Recipe - Servings: 2 (Makes 4 small pancakes or 2 large ones)

Ingredients:

Base (Energy & Protein Sources)

- Millet Flour (Ragi, Jowar, or Bajra) – ½ cup
- Eggs – 2
- Milk (or Plant-Based Alternative) – ¼ cup

Natural Energy Boosters

- Banana (Mashed, for sweetness & extra carbs) – 1 small
- Honey or Jaggery (Optional, for natural sugar boost) – 1 tsp

Healthy Fats & Nutrients

- Chia Seeds or Flaxseeds (Omega-3 & Fiber) – 1 tsp
- Almond Butter or Peanut Butter (For Sustained Energy) – 1 tbsp
- Ghee or Coconut Oil (For Cooking & Satiety) – 1 tsp

Flavour & Electrolyte Balance

- Cinnamon Powder (Stabilizes Blood Sugar Levels) – ½ tsp
- Turmeric Powder (Anti-Inflammatory, Optional) – ¼ tsp
- Salt (To Balance Electrolytes) – ¼ tsp

Step-by-Step Directions:

1. Prepare the Batter
    - In a bowl, whisk eggs and mashed banana until smooth.
    - Add millet flour, milk, cinnamon, turmeric, and salt, then mix well.
    - Stir in chia seeds and peanut butter to enhance texture and nutrition.
    - If the batter is too thick, add a little more milk to adjust consistency.
2. Cook the Pancakes
    - Heat a non-stick pan on medium heat and lightly grease it with ghee or coconut oil.
    - Pour small amounts of batter onto the pan and spread slightly.
    - Cook for 2-3 minutes per side until golden brown and firm.
    - Flip carefully and cook the other side for another 2 minutes.
3. Serve & Enjoy
    - Stack the pancakes and drizzle with honey, nut butter, or fresh fruit.
    - Enjoy warm for a satisfying, long-lasting energy boost.

Pari's Super Tip

"For extra protein, add a scoop of unflavored protein powder to the batter. Pair with Greek yogurt or a handful of nuts for even more muscle support."

Final Thoughts

This Millet & Egg Protein Pancake is more than just a pre-workout meal—it's a powerhouse of energy, endurance, and recovery. It fuels your body without sugar crashes, supports muscle function, and keeps you feeling strong throughout your workout.

"Fuel Smart, Train Hard – Millets Power Your Every Rep!"

The Recovery Window: Why Timing Matters for Post-Workout Nutrition

Post-workout nutrition isn't just about **what** you eat—it's also about **when** you eat. The period immediately after exercise, known as the **"Anabolic Window" or "Recovery Window,"** is crucial for **muscle repair, glycogen replenishment, and overall recovery.**

What is the Recovery Window?

The **Recovery Window** refers to the **30 to 60 minutes after exercise**, during which your body is highly responsive to nutrients. During this time:

- ☑ **Muscles absorb protein more efficiently** to repair microtears caused by exercise.
- ☑ **Glycogen stores are rapidly replenished**, restoring energy for future workouts.
- ☑ **Nutrients help reduce muscle inflammation**, minimizing post-exercise soreness.
- ☑ **Delayed recovery increases muscle fatigue and risk of injury** if nutrients are not provided.

Evidence-Based Insights

A 2018 study in the *Journal of the International Society of Sports Nutrition* found that **consuming protein and carbohydrates immediately post-exercise maximizes muscle recovery and performance gains.**

A 2017 review in *Sports Medicine* confirmed that **glycogen resynthesis is highest in the first 30 minutes post-exercise**, and delaying carbohydrate intake can slow down recovery.

A 2021 study in *Nutrients* highlighted that whole foods rich in **antioxidants, proteins, and complex carbs (such as millets)** aid in faster muscle repair compared to processed recovery drinks.

Pari's Super Tip:

"Think of post-workout recovery as part of your training—what you eat now determines how strong you perform tomorrow!"

The Best Foods for the Recovery Window

1. **Within 30 Minutes Post-Workout (Immediate Recovery)**
   - **Protein + Carbohydrates:** A 2:1 ratio of carbs to protein helps optimize muscle repair.
   - **Hydration:** Replenishing electrolytes prevents muscle cramps and dehydration.

   Examples:

   - **Ragi & Almond Milkshake** – Rich in calcium, protein, and natural sugars for energy.
   - **Banana with Millet Energy Balls** – A quick glycogen boost with healthy fats.
   - **Greek Yogurt with Millet Granola** – Protein-packed and gut-friendly.
2. **Within 60 Minutes Post-Workout (Deep Recovery & Growth Phase)**
   - **Balanced meal with lean protein, complex carbs, and healthy fats.**
   - **Antioxidants to reduce oxidative stress from intense exercise.**

   Examples:

   - **Millet Buddha Bowl with Grilled Chicken or Tofu** – A complete meal for muscle recovery.
   - **Kodo Millet "Fried Rice" with Egg or Paneer** – Ideal for sustained post-exercise energy.
   - **Ragi Pancakes with Nut Butter & Honey** – A delicious way to refuel.

Takeaway: Don't Miss the Recovery Window

- **Consume a well-balanced meal within 30–60 minutes post-exercise** for optimal muscle repair and energy replenishment.
- **Include protein, complex carbs, and hydration** to enhance strength and prevent soreness.
- **Whole foods like millets, nuts, and dairy** provide natural, sustained recovery benefits compared to processed supplements.

Recipe 7 – Kodo Millet & Grilled Chicken Bowl –

Sustained recovery and strength building

Why This Works:

- **Kodo Millet** is rich in **antioxidants, fibre, and slow-digesting carbs**, making it ideal for **sustained energy release.**
- **Grilled Chicken** provides **lean protein** for muscle repair.
- **Avocado & Nuts** add **healthy fats**, reducing post-workout inflammation.
- **Leafy Greens & Vegetables** help replenish **electrolytes & minerals.**

Recipe - Servings: 2

Ingredients:

Base (Carb & Fiber Source)

- **Kodo Millet (Cooked & Fluffy)** – 1 cup

Protein & Recovery Boosters

- **Grilled Chicken Breast (Sliced)** – ½ cup
- *(Vegetarian Option: Replace with **grilled paneer or tofu**)

Vegetables & Electrolytes

- **Spinach or Kale (For Iron & Magnesium)** – ½ cup
- **Cherry Tomatoes (Rich in Antioxidants)** – ¼ cup, halved
- **Cucumber (For Hydration & Freshness)** – ¼ cup, chopped

Healthy Fats & Extras

- **Avocado (For Omega-3 & Good Fats)** – ½ small, sliced
- **Almonds or Walnuts (For Crunch & Extra Protein)** – 1 tbsp, chopped
- **Olive Oil (For Flavor & Healthy Fats)** – 1 tsp

Dressing (For Taste & Recovery Benefits)

- **Greek Yogurt (For Extra Protein & Probiotics)** – 2 tbsp
- **Lemon Juice (For Vitamin C & Absorption)** – 1 tbsp
- **Salt & Black Pepper (For Flavor & Electrolyte Balance)** – To taste

Step-by-Step Directions:

1. **Cook the Kodo Millet**
   - Rinse **½ cup Kodo millet** and cook with **1 cup water** until soft and fluffy.
   - Let it cool before assembling the bowl.
2. **Grill the Chicken (or Paneer/Tofu)**
   - Marinate **chicken breast (or tofu/paneer)** with **lemon juice, olive oil, salt, and pepper.**
   - Grill on a **medium flame for 5-7 minutes per side** until fully cooked.
3. **Prepare the Dressing**
   - Mix **Greek yogurt, lemon juice, salt, and black pepper** for a creamy dressing.
4. **Assemble the Bowl**
   - Start with a base of **Kodo millet.**
   - Add **grilled chicken slices, chopped vegetables, and avocado.**
   - Sprinkle with **chopped nuts and drizzle with dressing.**
5. **Serve & Enjoy**
   - Toss everything lightly and enjoy a **power-packed recovery meal.**

Best Time to Consume: Within 60 minutes post-workout for **deep muscle recovery and sustained energy.**

Final Thoughts: Why These Millet Meals Matter Post-Workout

✓ **Balanced Macronutrients** – Carbs, protein, and healthy fats in the right ratio.

✓ **Natural & Whole Ingredients** – No processed supplements, only real food.

✓ **Muscle Recovery & Strength Building** – Essential for long-term fitness goals.

✓ **Electrolyte & Mineral Replenishment** – Reduces fatigue, cramps, and soreness.

Pari's Super Tip:

"Post-workout recovery isn't just about refueling—it's about preparing your body for the next challenge. Make every meal count!"

Recipe 8 – Pearl Millet (Bajra) & Berry Protein Smoothie

Post-Workout Recovery Drink

Bajra (pearl millet) is rich in magnesium, which helps relax muscles and prevent cramps. A **perfect blend of protein, healthy carbs, and antioxidants**, this **Bajra & Berry Smoothie** is designed to **repair muscles, replenish glycogen, and reduce post-exercise inflammation.**

Recipe - Servings: 2

Ingredients:

Base (Millet & Protein Source)

- **Bajra (Pearl Millet) Flour** – 2 tbsp *(Pre-cooked & cooled for better digestion)*
- **Greek Yogurt (For Probiotics & Extra Protein)** – ½ cup

Carb & Energy Boosters

- **Banana (For Natural Sugars & Potassium)** – 1 small
- **Mixed Berries (Blueberries, Strawberries, or Raspberries)** – ½ cup

Healthy Fats & Electrolytes

- **Almonds (Soaked & Blended)** – 6-8
- **Chia Seeds (For Omega-3 & Hydration Support)** – 1 tsp

Flavor & Recovery Boosters

- **Cinnamon Powder (Anti-Inflammatory & Blood Sugar Control)** – ½ tsp
- **Honey or Jaggery Syrup (Optional, for Extra Sweetness)** – 1 tsp

Cold Water or Almond Milk (For Blending & Smooth Consistency) – 1 cup

Step-by-Step Directions:

1. **Pre-Cook the Bajra Flour**
    - Mix **2 tbsp bajra flour with ½ cup water** and heat on low flame for **3-4 minutes** until smooth.
    - Let it cool completely before using in the smoothie.
2. **Blend the Ingredients**
    - In a blender, add **cooked bajra paste, Greek yogurt, banana, berries, almonds, chia seeds, cinnamon, and honey.**
    - Pour in **cold water or almond milk** and blend until smooth.
3. **Serve & Enjoy**
    - Pour into a glass and **chill for a refreshing post-workout boost.**
    - Optionally, **garnish with a few extra berries or crushed almonds.**

Best Time to Consume:

- **Within 30-60 minutes post-exercise** for **muscle recovery, electrolyte balance, and glycogen replenishment.**

Why This Smoothie is Great for Post-Workout Recovery

☑ **Bajra (Pearl Millet) is rich in magnesium & fiber** – Supports muscle relaxation and digestion.

☑ **Greek Yogurt & Almonds add high-quality protein** – Essential for muscle repair.

☑ **Berries provide antioxidants & Vitamin C** – Helps fight inflammation and oxidative stress.

☑ **Chia Seeds for Omega-3 & Electrolytes** – Reduces muscle soreness and enhances hydration.

☑ **Banana for Natural Sugars & Potassium** – Replenishes glycogen stores and prevents cramps.

Pari's Super Tip:

"For a thicker smoothie bowl, reduce liquid and top with sliced bananas, chia seeds, and granola!"

SUCCESS STORY – 2

"From Burnout to Beast Mode: Arjun's 30-Day Transformation with Alamirap!"

Arjun was like most young professionals—overworked, stressed, and constantly exhausted. At 28, he had a promising career in IT, decent pay, and a life that seemed stable. But underneath it all, he was running on empty. Late nights spent debugging code meant skipping breakfast in the morning. Lunch breaks were a blur of fast-food deliveries—pizza, burgers, and sodas.

Evenings? He wanted to work out, but his body had other plans.

He tried hitting the gym after work, but most days, he ended up on the couch, too drained to even think about exercise. *"I'll start next week,"* he told himself. But weeks turned into months. One evening, as he struggled to climb a flight of stairs without losing his breath, he realized something was seriously wrong.

That night, he searched online for ways to boost energy naturally. And that's when he came across AlaMirap Nutrition.

A Leap of Faith: The Alamirap Consultation

At first, Arjun was like most of us. Resistant to change.

"Can food really make that much of a difference?" he wondered.

But he had tried everything else—protein shakes, caffeine, crash diets—and nothing had worked. So he decided to reach out. During his first consultation with AlaMirap Nutrition, we didn't talk about weight loss or gym routines.

We talked about something far more important—energy.

"Your body isn't broken, Arjun," I told him. *"It's just running on the wrong fuel."*

He was intrigued. We didn't force drastic changes. Instead, we suggested one simple experiment:

- [x] For 30 days, cook dinner at home using millets every weekday.

That's it. No extreme restrictions, no calorie counting.

Just one small commitment – for the next 30 days.

Week 1: Breaking Old Habits

The first week was tough. Cooking at home felt like a chore. It was easier to order food, just like he always had. But he had promised himself 30 days.

His first meal? A simple foxtail millet stir-fry with vegetables and paneer.

Not bad. By day four, he tried millet porridge with lentils, a dish his grandmother used to make. Something shifted—he started feeling lighter. The usual bloated, sluggish feeling after meals? Gone. And for the first time in months, he woke up without hitting snooze ten times.

Week 2: The Energy Surge

By the second week, Arjun noticed something strange.

- [x] He wasn't craving junk food anymore.
- [x] He felt more energetic in the evenings.
- [x] And one day, without even planning it, he went to the gym.

It wasn't a long session—just a 20-minute jog on the treadmill.

But it was the first time in months he had enough energy to even attempt a workout after work.

Week 3: Visible Changes

By now, the results were impossible to ignore.

His clothes? Looser.

His cravings? Under control.

His gym sessions? More consistent.

He realized he didn't need cheat meals—because he wasn't "dieting." He was simply fuelling his body differently.

- ☑ Bajra roti with dal instead of naan.
- ☑ Foxtail millet upma instead of noodles.
- ☑ Kodo millet pulao instead of white rice.

And the best part? No crash. No sluggishness.

His body felt fuelled, not overloaded.

Week 4: A New Arjun

By the end of 30 days, the transformation was undeniable.

His waist had dropped by 5 cm.

His energy levels had skyrocketed.

And his gym performance had improved effortlessly.

For the first time, he felt in control.

One evening, while tying his shoelaces before a workout, he looked in the mirror and saw something he hadn't seen in a long time—determination.

This wasn't just about getting fit.

This was about getting his life back.

One Year Later: Arjun 2.0

Today, Arjun isn't just another IT guy complaining about fatigue and work stress.

He's the guy who completed his first 10K run.

The guy who chooses food that fuels him, not food that drains him.

The guy who swapped his Netflix marathons for actual marathons.

"Abs are made in the kitchen," he laughs, *"and millets gave me the nutrition I needed without excess calories. I build muscle faster now and don't miss my old junk food at all."*

The Alamirap Way: Small Changes, Big Results

Arjun's story isn't unique.

Most young professionals feel exhausted, sluggish, and drained. Not because they're lazy. Not because they don't try, but because they're fuelling their bodies the wrong way.

☑ One small habit change transformed Arjun's life. All it takes is a CHOICE

> *"The best decision I ever made? Giving my body what it truly needed. The rest fell into place."* – Arjun

Chapter 4

DIABETES AND MILLETS: RECLAIMING HEALTH, ONE GRAIN AT A TIME

Diabetes is no longer a disease of the elderly. It is creeping into the lives of young adults, teenagers, and even children at an alarming rate.

With India being the diabetes capital of the world, millions of families are watching their loved ones struggle with high blood sugar, constant fatigue, and lifelong medication.

The worst part? Most of these cases are preventable.

The solution doesn't lie in fancy supplements or expensive treatments. It lies in what we eat, how we move, and how we take care of ourselves daily.

And in this fight, millets are one of our strongest weapons.

The Burden of Diabetes in India: Where Are We Headed?

* India has over 101 million adults living with diabetes, and another 136 million with prediabetes (ICMR-INDIAB study, 2023).
* One in every six diabetics in the world is an Indian.
* Type 2 diabetes is now affecting people as young as 25.
* Children are being diagnosed with prediabetes due to poor diet and lack of physical activity.

And these numbers aren't just statistics—they represent millions of lives being disrupted.

Diabetes doesn't just raise blood sugar levels—it damages nerves, weakens eyesight, increases heart risks, and affects kidney health.

But here's the most empowering truth:

Type 2 diabetes is largely preventable, and in many cases, reversible with lifestyle changes.

How Early Should Intervention Start?

The biggest mistake that people make!

Waiting for a diagnosis before taking action. We often think diabetes happens to "older people" or "unhealthy people." But in reality:

- ☑ Prediabetes can start silently in the 20s and 30s.
- ☑ By the time someone is diagnosed, years of damage have already begun.
- ☑ Unhealthy childhood habits set the stage for diabetes later in life.

That's why intervention should start early.

Children, young adults, and families need to make small but powerful shifts—not just to avoid diabetes, but to build a foundation of lifelong health.

Ways to Prevent or Manage Diabetes and Address early-stage insulin resistance

Diabetes prevention isn't about avoiding sugar alone. It's about changing our lifestyle, one habit at a time.

- ☑ Eating Smart:
  - Choose whole grains like millets over white rice and refined flours.
  - Increase fiber intake with vegetables, nuts, and seeds.
  - Reduce processed carbs and deep-fried foods.
- ☑ Moving More:
  - Exercise for at least 30 minutes daily—even a simple walk helps.
  - Avoid sitting for long hours—take movement breaks every 45 minutes.
  - Incorporate strength training to improve insulin sensitivity.
- ☑ Managing Stress:
  - High stress increases blood sugar. Make time for meditation, yoga, or hobbies.
  - Prioritize sleep—less than 6 hours of sleep raises diabetes risk.

☑ Mindful Eating Habits:

- Eat slowly, chew well, and stop when 80% full.
- Fix meal timings—erratic eating patterns spike blood sugar.
- Stay hydrated—water helps regulate blood sugar levels.

Millets: A Superfood for Diabetes Control

Millets are one of the most effective grains for diabetes management—and science backs this up.

📌 A 2021 study published in the journal *Frontiers in Nutrition* found that millets can reduce fasting blood sugar levels by 12-15% and improve insulin sensitivity.

📌 Another study in the *British Journal of Nutrition* confirmed that replacing white rice with millets significantly lowers post-meal blood sugar spikes.

Why are millets so effective for diabetes?

☑ Low Glycemic Index (GI): Unlike white rice and wheat, millets release glucose slowly into the bloodstream, preventing sugar spikes.

☑ High Fiber: Keeps you full for longer and stabilizes blood sugar levels.

☑ Rich in Magnesium & Zinc: Helps insulin function properly.

☑ Complex Carbohydrates: Provide sustained energy without sugar crashes.

☑ Gluten-Free & Anti-Inflammatory: Supports gut health, which is crucial for metabolism and sugar control.

Diabetes-Friendly Diet – Smart swaps without sacrificing your favourite foods

☑ Replace White Rice with Millets

- Swap foxtail millet, little millet, or barnyard millet in place of rice.
- Try millet pulao, khichdi, or curd millet instead of white rice meals.

- ☑ Choose Millet-Based Breakfasts
  - Ragi dosa instead of white flour dosas.
  - Jowar or Bajra roti instead of regular wheat roti.
  - Millet porridge or upma instead of bread-based breakfasts.
- ☑ Snack Smart
  - Millet-based energy balls with nuts and seeds.
  - Roasted jowar or bajra puffs instead of deep-fried snacks.
- ☑ Try Diabetes-Friendly Millet Desserts
  - Ragi laddoos with jaggery instead of sugar-loaded sweets.
  - Millet kheer with almond milk instead of rice-based kheer.

Recipe 9 – Little Millet Vegetable Upma (A Fiber-Rich Start to the Day)

Why This Works

- **Little millet** has a **low glycemic index**, which helps regulate blood sugar levels.
- **Vegetables add fiber** to slow down glucose absorption.
- **Ghee improves satiety** and aids digestion.

Ingredients (Serves 2):

- **Little Millet** – ½ cup
- **Water** – 1 ½ cups
- **Carrot, Beans, Capsicum (Finely Chopped)** – ½ cup
- **Ghee** – 1 tsp
- **Mustard Seeds** – ½ tsp
- **Curry Leaves** – 4-5
- **Ginger (Grated)** – ½ tsp
- **Green Chili (Chopped, Optional)** – 1
- **Salt** – To taste **Turmeric Powder** – ¼ tsp

Directions:

1. Dry roast the little millet for 2 minutes until fragrant. Set aside.
2. Heat ghee in a pan, add mustard seeds, curry leaves, ginger, and green chili. Sauté for a few seconds.
3. Add chopped vegetables and cook for 2 minutes.
4. Add water, turmeric, and salt, and bring to a boil.
5. Stir in the roasted millet, cover, and cook for 8-10 minutes on low flame until the water is absorbed. Fluff with a fork and serve warm.

Recipe 10 – Proso Millet & Flaxseed Pancakes (Protein-Packed Stable Energy Release)

Why This Works:

- **Proso millet** is **high in protein**, preventing sugar spikes.
- **Flaxseeds add omega-3 fatty acids**, which improve insulin sensitivity.
- **Greek yogurt enhances gut health**, which is essential for glucose control.

Ingredients (Serves 2):

- **Proso Millet Flour** – ½ cup
- **Eggs** – 2 (or Flaxseed Egg – 2 tbsp flaxseed powder + 5 tbsp water)
- **Greek Yogurt** – ¼ cup
- **Cinnamon Powder** – ½ tsp
- **Honey (Optional, for mild sweetness)** – 1 tsp
- **Milk or Almond Milk** – ¼ cup
- **Ghee** – 1 tsp for cooking

Directions:

1. In a bowl, whisk eggs (or flaxseed egg) with Greek yogurt, honey, and cinnamon.
2. Slowly add the proso millet flour and milk, whisking until smooth.
3. Heat a pan with ghee and pour small portions of batter. Cook until bubbles appear, flip, and cook for another 2 minutes.
4. Serve warm with nuts or a drizzle of almond butter.

Fun Fact:

Proso millet is like the **slow-release energy drink of grains**—it keeps your blood sugar steady, so no energy crashes, just all-day power! It has a **lower glycemic index than white rice**, meaning it **won't spike your blood sugar**—so you can stay fuelled without the sugar crash!

Recipe 11 – Browntop Millet & Stir-Fry Noodles (A Healthy Take on Comfort Food)

Why This Works:

- **Browntop millet is gluten-free and high in fiber**, making it an excellent substitute for refined noodles. Vegetables and protein slow down glucose release.

Ingredients (Serves 2): Millet Noodles are available in regular stores

- **Browntop Millet Noodles** – 1 cup
- **Capsicum, Carrot, Spring Onion (Julienned)** – ½ cup
- **Tofu or Grilled Chicken (For Protein)** – ½ cup
- **Garlic (Minced)** – 2 cloves
- **Soy Sauce** – 1 tbsp
- **Sesame Oil** – 1 tsp
- **Black Pepper** – ½ tsp

Directions:

1. Boil browntop millet noodles or cook until soft.
2. Heat sesame oil in a pan, add garlic, and sauté for 30 seconds.
3. Add vegetables/tofu/cooked chicken and stir fry for few minutes.
4. Add cooked millet/noodles, soy sauce, and black pepper. Toss well and serve.

Why Millet Noodles Are Superior to Instant Noodles

☑ Low Glycemic Index & Blood Sugar Friendly – Unlike instant noodles, which cause sugar spikes, millet noodles release energy slowly, keeping you full longer and preventing crashes.

☑ No Preservatives, No MSG – Readymade instant noodles are packed with preservatives, artificial flavor enhancers (MSG), and unhealthy additives, whereas millet noodles are natural, fiber-rich, and gut-friendly.

☑ More Protein & Fiber, Less Empty Carbs – Millet noodles contain higher protein and fiber content, supporting muscle recovery and digestion, while instant noodles are mostly refined flour (maida) with little to no nutrition.

Recipe 12 – Foxtail Millet & Lentil Khichdi (A Comforting One-Pot Meal)

Why This Works:

- Foxtail millet and lentils create a balanced protein-carb meal.
- Turmeric and ginger improve insulin function.

Ingredients (Serves 2):

- **Foxtail Millet** – ½ cup
- **Moong Dal (Lentils)** – ¼ cup
- **Turmeric Powder** – ¼ tsp
- **Ginger (Grated)** – 1 tsp
- **Ghee** – 1 tsp
- **Cumin Seeds** – ½ tsp

Directions:

1. Rinse and soak millet and dal for 30 minutes.
2. In a pressure cooker, heat ghee, add cumin and ginger.
3. Add millet, dal, turmeric, and 2 cups water. Cook for 3 whistles.
4. Serve warm with yogurt.

3 Ways to Make Foxtail Millet More Diabetic-Friendly

1. **Pair with Protein & Healthy Fats** – Combine foxtail millet with **lentils, nuts, seeds, or paneer** to **slow down glucose absorption** and enhance satiety.
2. **Use Minimal Processing** – Opt for **whole foxtail millet** instead of refined versions to retain fibre and nutrients. Avoid overcooking to maintain a low GI.
3. **Add Low-GI Vegetables** – Incorporate **leafy greens, bell peppers, and bitter gourd** into foxtail millet dishes to **further stabilise blood sugar levels.**

"Balance your plate, not just your blood sugar—let foxtail millet nourish you with steady energy, fibre, and natural goodness."

Recipe 13 – Ragi Mudde (Finger Millet Balls) – A Power-Packed Staple of Karnataka

Ingredients - Traditional Ragi Mudde Recipe (Serves 2)

- **1 cup ragi (finger millet) flour**
- **2 cups water**
- **½ teaspoon salt**
- **1 teaspoon ghee (optional, for flavour and smoothness)**

Step-by-Step Method

Step 1: Boil Water

- In a heavy-bottomed pan, **bring 2 cups of water to a boil**.
- Add **½ teaspoon salt** and **1 teaspoon ghee** (optional).

Step 2: Prepare the Ragi Mixture

- Take **¼ cup of ragi flour** and mix it with **¼ cup of water** in a separate bowl to make a lump-free paste.
- Slowly pour this mixture into the boiling water while stirring continuously.

Step 3: Cook the Ragi Flour

- Gradually add the **remaining ragi flour** to the pan while **stirring vigorously** with a wooden spoon (avoid lumps).
- Reduce the heat to **low** and cover with a lid for **2-3 minutes** to allow steam to cook the flour.

Step 4: Knead and Shape the Mudde

- Once the mixture thickens and starts leaving the sides of the pan, turn off the heat.
- Wet your hands slightly, scoop a portion, and shape it into **smooth, round balls**.

Step 5: Serve Hot

- Traditionally, Ragi Mudde is **swallowed, not chewed**, and served with **soppu saaru (leafy greens curry)**, **rasam**, or **spicy chicken curry**.

Health Benefits of Ragi Mudde

Ragi Mudde, a **staple in Karnataka**, has been a favourite among farmers, athletes, and health-conscious individuals for centuries. Known for its **high energy content** and **sustained release of nutrients**, this humble dish is a powerhouse of **calcium, iron, and dietary fibre**.

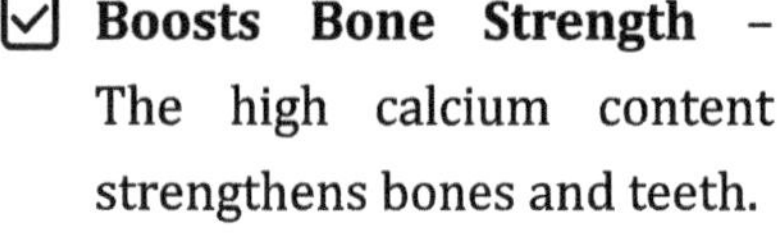

☑ **Boosts Bone Strength** – The high calcium content strengthens bones and teeth.

☑ **Aids in Weight Loss** – Keeps you full for longer and reduces cravings.

☑ **Improves Digestion** – Rich in fibre, it promotes a healthy gut.

☑ **Great for Diabetes Control** – Helps regulate blood sugar levels.

Interesting Facts About Ragi

- **Calcium King** – Ragi has **10 times more calcium than rice and wheat**, making it excellent for **bone health** and **osteoporosis prevention.**
- **Natural Protein Source** – It contains **essential amino acids** that aid **muscle repair and growth.**
- **Gluten-Free & Diabetic-Friendly** – Its **low glycaemic index (GI)** ensures **slow glucose release**, helping **control blood sugar spikes**.

Recipe 14 – Ragi Slurry for Babies (Finger millet Porridge) – Toddlers Recipe

Ingredients:

- **2 tbsp ragi flour**
- **1 cup water**
- **½ tsp ghee (optional, for taste and digestion aid)**
- **Jaggery / Dates puree (optional, for mild sweetness)**

Step-by-Step Preparation

1. **Soak & Sprout (Optional, for Better Nutrition)** – Soak ragi overnight and allow it to sprout for 12-24 hours. Dry and grind into fine flour.
2. **Make a Slurry** – In a small pan, mix **2 tbsp of ragi flour** with **½ cup of water**, ensuring no lumps.
3. **Cook Slowly** – Heat the mixture on low flame, stirring continuously. Add the remaining water gradually.
4. **Enhance with Ghee & Sweetener** – Once it thickens (after 5 minutes), add **½ tsp ghee** for better digestion. If needed, add a small amount of **jaggery or dates puree**.
5. **Cool & Serve** – Let it cool slightly before feeding the baby. **No sugar or salt** should be added for babies under **one year old**.
    - **Easily Digestible** – The high fibre and smooth texture make it **gentle on a baby's stomach**.
    - **Iron-Rich** – Helps **prevent anaemia** in growing toddlers.
    - **Calcium Powerhouse** – Strengthens **bones and teeth** in the early stages of development.
    - **Natural Gluten-Free Option** – Ideal for babies with **sensitive digestion**.
    - It's **never too early** to introduce kids to millets! Start young, build stronger bones, and fuel their future with the power of ancient grains.

- **Master the art of rotating carbohydrates**! From rice to ragi, foxtail to bajra—diversity in grains means balanced nutrition for growing minds and bodies."

Did You Know?

What is the First Preferred Food to Introduce to Toddlers?

When babies turn **6 months old**, their nutritional needs change, and **breast milk alone isn't enough**. The first solid food introduced mostly in entire generations of my family has been:

> **"Ragi Slurry – The Tiny Tummy Super Fuel! Packed with calcium, iron, and love in every spoon!"**

Recipe 15 – Jowar Roti (Sorghum Flatbread)

Jowar roti, also known as Jolad Roti in Karnataka and Maharashtra, is a staple in many Indian households. This soft, gluten-free flatbread is packed with nutrients and provides sustained energy.

Step-by-Step Recipe: Jowar Roti (Makes 4 Rotis)

Ingredients:

✓ 1 cup jowar (sorghum) flour

✓ ¾ cup hot water (adjust as needed)

✓ ½ tsp salt (optional)

✓ Dry flour for dusting

Step-by-Step Method

Step 1: Prepare the Dough

1. Heat ¾ cup water until warm (not boiling).
2. In a bowl, add jowar flour and salt. Slowly pour the warm water while mixing.
3. Knead into a smooth, soft dough (jowar lacks gluten, so knead gently). Cover and rest for 5 minutes.

Step 2: Rolling the Roti

4. Take a small portion of dough and dust with dry flour.
5. Place on a rolling board and gently flatten using your fingers or a rolling pin. If it cracks, moisten hands and reshape.
6. Ensure it's thin and even (about 6 inches in diameter).

Step 3: Cooking the Roti

7. Heat a tawa (griddle) on medium-high flame.
8. Carefully place the roti and cook for 30 seconds until bubbles appear.
9. Flip and cook for another 30 seconds, pressing lightly with a cloth.
10. Flip again and cook directly on the flame for puffing (optional).

Step 4: Serve Hot

11. Brush with ghee for extra softness and flavour.
12. Serve with dal, sabzi, or chutney for a wholesome meal!

Recipe 16 – Bajra Khichdi (Pearl Millet Khichdi) – A High-Protein, Diabetes-Friendly Recipe

Bajra (Pearl Millet) Khichdi is a **nutrient-dense, gluten-free**, and **gut-friendly** dish, commonly eaten in Rajasthan and Gujarat. With its **low glycaemic index (GI ~ 55)** and high **fibre and protein content**, this wholesome one-pot meal is perfect for **diabetics, weight watchers, and muscle building**.

Step-by-Step Recipe: Bajra Khichdi (Serves 2-3)

Interesting Facts About Bajra (Pearl Millet)

- **Rich in Protein** – Contains **12-14g protein per 100g**, making it a great plant-based protein source.
- **Gut-Friendly** – High in **insoluble fibre**, aids digestion, and promotes gut health.
- **Heart-Healthy** – Loaded with **magnesium & potassium**, helps in reducing blood pressure.
- **Diabetic-Friendly** – Its **slow digestion rate** prevents blood sugar spikes.

Ingredients:

- **½ cup bajra (pearl millet), soaked overnight**
- **¼ cup yellow moong dal (split lentils)**
- **4 cups water**
- **½ tsp turmeric powder**
- **1 tsp ghee (or oil for a vegan option)**
- **1 tsp cumin seeds**
- **1 small onion, chopped**
- **1 small tomato, chopped**
- **1 small carrot, diced** (optional, for added fibre)
- **½ cup spinach, finely chopped** (optional, for iron boost)
- **1 green chilli, chopped** (adjust to taste)
- **1 tsp grated ginger**
- **Salt to taste**

Preparation Method

1. **Prepare the Bajra**
   - Soak **½ cup bajra overnight** for better digestibility.
   - Drain, rinse, and **coarsely crush** it using a mortar-pestle or a blender.
2. **Cook the Lentils and Bajra**
   - In a pressure cooker or pot, add **bajra, moong dal, 4 cups water, turmeric, and salt**.
   - Pressure cook for **3-4 whistles** (or **25-30 mins in a pan** on low heat) until soft.
3. **Tempering (Tadka) for Flavour**
   - Heat **1 tsp ghee** in a pan, add **cumin seeds**, let them splutter.
   - Add **onions, green chilli, and ginger**. Sauté until golden brown.
   - Toss in **tomatoes, carrots, and spinach**, sauté for 2-3 minutes.
4. **Combine Everything**
   - Add the cooked **bajra and dal mixture** into the pan and mix well.
   - Adjust water consistency, simmer for **5 minutes**, and stir occasionally.
5. **Serve Hot**
   - Garnish with **fresh coriander & a squeeze of lemon juice** for extra freshness.
   - Serve with **curd or mint chutney** for added flavour.

Ways to Increase Protein Content

Add Sprouted Moong – Toss in **½ cup sprouted moong** after cooking for a **protein boost**.

Egg White Topping – Stir in **2 egg whites** while simmering for extra **lean protein**.

Nut & Seed Power – Add **flaxseeds, sesame, or almonds** for crunch & nutrients.

How to Make It More Diabetic-Friendly

- ☑ **Add Fibre-Rich Veggies – broccoli, bell peppers, and methi (fenugreek leaves)**.
- ☑ **Pair with Curd or Buttermilk** – This **lowers the glycaemic load** of the meal.
- ☑ **Skip the Ghee (or Use in Moderation)** – Keeps it heart-healthy and light.

Recipe 17 – Tantalizing High-Protein Foxtail Millet Upma

This isn't your regular upma—it's a protein-rich, nutty, and flavourful twist on a classic South Indian dish! Made with foxtail millet (thinai), loaded with plant-based protein, healthy fats, and aromatic spices, this upma is perfect for muscle recovery, gut health, and sustained energy.

Why Foxtail Millet? 🌾

- **High Protein (12g per 100g) – Great for muscle repair & satiety.**
- **Diabetic-Friendly (Low GI ~ 50) – Keeps blood sugar stable.**
- **Rich in Iron & B-Vitamins – Boosts stamina & brain function.**

Step-by-Step Recipe: Protein-Packed Foxtail Millet Upma (Serves 2-3)

Ingredients:

- 1 cup foxtail millet (Navane/thinai), soaked for 30 mins
- ½ cup sprouted moong dal (or boiled chickpeas/lentils) – For extra protein
- 2 tbsp ghee – Adds healthy fats & rich flavour
- 2 tbsp grated coconut – For a creamy texture & essential fats
- 1 tsp mustard seeds
- 1 tsp cumin seeds
- 1 small onion, finely chopped
- 1-inch ginger, grated
- 1 green chilli, chopped (adjust spice level)
- 6-8 curry leaves
- ½ cup chopped vegetables (carrots, bell peppers, spinach)
- 2 cups hot water
- Salt to taste
- ½ tsp turmeric powder
- ½ tsp black pepper (optional for metabolism boost)
- Juice of ½ lemon (for a fresh zing)
- Handful of roasted cashews (for crunch & extra protein)

Preparation Method

Step 1: Dry Roast the Millet

- In a dry pan, roast foxtail millet on medium heat for 2-3 minutes until aromatic.
- This enhances the nutty flavour and makes the upma fluffier.

Step 2: Ghee Tempering (Tadka)

- Heat 2 tbsp ghee in a pan, add mustard & cumin seeds—let them splutter.
- Toss in curry leaves, green chilli, ginger, and onions. Sauté until onions turn translucent.

Step 3: Add Protein & Vegetables

- Stir in sprouted moong dal, chopped veggies, turmeric, black pepper, and salt.
- Sauté for 3-4 minutes until veggies slightly soften but remain crunchy.

Step 4: Cooking the Millet

- Add hot water (2 cups) and roasted foxtail millet, mix well.
- Cover and simmer on low flame for 8-10 minutes, stirring occasionally.
- Once the millet absorbs water and becomes fluffy, turn off the heat.

Step 5: Finish with Coconut & Cashews

- Mix in grated coconut for a creamy texture and natural sweetness.
- Garnish with roasted cashews and a squeeze of fresh lemon juice for the perfect balance of crunch and tang!

Why This Upma is Next-Level Amazing

☑ Protein-Packed – Lentils, millet & nuts = Complete protein profile.

☑ Rich in Healthy Fats – Ghee + Coconut = Gut-friendly and long-lasting energy.

☑ Full of Fiber & Nutrients – Keeps you full longer and improves digestion.

Serve Hot! Enjoy with coconut chutney, raita, or a cup of herbal tea for a satisfying and balanced meal!

"Upma: The Comforting Hug of Flavours in Every Bite!"

Recipe 18 – Sugar-Free Ragi Muffins

A Guilt-Free Indulgence for Beginners!

Who says diabetics must give up sweets? With the right ingredients, you can enjoy delicious treats without sugar spikes!

Easy Sugar-Free Ragi Muffins Recipe (Beginner-Friendly, Makes 6 Muffins)

Ingredients:

- 1 cup ragi (finger millet) flour
- ½ cup rolled oats (powdered) – for extra fibre
- 1 tsp baking powder
- ½ tsp baking soda
- ½ tsp cinnamon powder (optional, for flavour & blood sugar control)
- ¼ cup mashed banana OR 3 tbsp dates paste (natural sweetener)
- ¼ cup unsweetened Greek yogurt (for moisture & protein)
- ¼ cup milk (or almond milk for dairy-free option)
- 1 tbsp melted coconut oil OR ghee
- ½ tsp vanilla extract (optional)
- 2 tbsp chopped nuts (almonds, walnuts, or sunflower seeds)

Step-by-Step Instructions

Step 1: Preheat & Prepare

- Preheat oven to 180°C (350°F).
- Line a muffin tray with paper liners or grease lightly with coconut oil.

Step 2: Mix Dry Ingredients

- In a bowl, whisk together ragi flour, oat flour, baking powder, baking soda, and cinnamon.

Step 3: Combine Wet Ingredients

- In another bowl, mash banana (or mix dates paste).
- Add Greek yogurt, milk, melted coconut oil, and vanilla extract. Mix well.

Step 4: Make the Batter

- Slowly fold the wet mixture into the dry ingredients.
- Add chopped nuts and gently mix (do not overmix).

Step 5: Bake the Muffins

- Pour batter into muffin cups, filling ¾ of the way.
- Bake for 15-18 minutes or until a toothpick comes out clean.

Step 6: Cool & Enjoy

- Let muffins cool for 5-10 minutes before removing from the tray.
- Enjoy warm or store in an airtight container for up to 3 days.

These soft, fluffy, and naturally sweetened Ragi (Finger Millet) Muffins are packed with fibre, protein, and healthy fats—perfect for a diabetic-friendly snack.

Why These Ragi Muffins Are Perfect for Diabetics

✓ Naturally Sweetened – No refined sugar, only low-GI natural sweeteners.

✓ High in Fibre & Protein – Helps control sugar spikes and keeps you full longer.

✓ Gluten-Free & Nutrient-Dense – Ragi provides calcium, iron, and antioxidants.

Smart Swaps for Diabetics – Enjoy Sweets the Right Way!

- ☑ Choose Natural Sweeteners – Use dates, mashed bananas, or stevia instead of refined sugar to keep it low-GI.
- ☑ Switch to Whole Grains – Replace refined flour with ragi, oats, or almond flour for sustained energy and better digestion.
- ☑ Add Healthy Fats & Protein – Use nuts, seeds, and Greek yogurt to balance blood sugar levels.

Recipe 19 – Little Millet Payasam

A Diabetic-Friendly Twist on a Classic Sweet

Traditional payasam (kheer) is delicious but often loaded with sugar and high-GI ingredients. This Little Millet Payasam is gut-friendly, rich in protein and fibre, and naturally sweetened for stable blood sugar levels. Plus, it's so delicious that the entire family can enjoy it without guilt!

How to Make This Payasam Better Than Regular Sweet Porridge?

☑ Boost Protein & Fibre – Add moong dal and coconut milk to improve digestion and satiety.

☑ Use the Right Sweetener – Dates, monk fruit, or stevia are excellent low-GI options for diabetics.

☑ Enhance Taste Without Sugar – Use cardamom, saffron, and toasted nuts to bring depth and richness.

Best Natural Sweeteners for Diabetics (Low GI & Nutrient-Rich)

✓ Dates Paste (GI ~ 42) – Adds natural caramel-like sweetness and iron.

✓ Monk Fruit Extract (GI ~ 0) – A zero-GI natural sweetener with a mild taste.

✓ Stevia (Pure Extract) (GI ~ 0) – Sweetness without affecting blood sugar levels.

Step-by-Step Recipe: Diabetic-Friendly Little Millet Payasam

Ingredients (Serves 3-4)

- ½ cup little millet (samai), washed & soaked for 30 mins
- ¼ cup moong dal (yellow lentils), dry roasted – for added protein
- 2 cups water
- ½ cup coconut milk (thick, unsweetened) – for natural creaminess & healthy fats
- ½ tsp cardamom powder – enhances flavour naturally
- 2 tbsp grated coconut – adds richness without sugar
- 1 tbsp ghee – for taste & gut health
- 2 tbsp dates paste OR monk fruit extract (as per preference)
- 10 almonds & 5 cashews, toasted & chopped – for crunch & nutrition
- A few saffron strands (optional) – adds a luxurious touch

Preparation Method

Step 1: Cook Millet & Moong Dal

- Heat 1 cup water in a pan, add dry roasted moong dal and cook for 5 minutes.
- Add soaked little millet and 1 more cup of water. Cook on low flame for 10 minutcs, stirring occasionally until soft.

Step 2: Infuse Flavours

- Once the millet and dal are well-cooked, add coconut milk, cardamom powder, grated coconut, and saffron strands.
- Simmer for 5 minutes (don't boil coconut milk to avoid curdling).

Step 3: Sweeten Naturally

- Stir in dates paste OR monk fruit extract and mix well.
- Cook for 2-3 minutes to blend the flavours.

Step 4: Toast & Garnish

- In a small pan, heat 1 tbsp ghee, roast almonds and cashews until golden brown.
- Pour over the payasam and mix gently.

How to Ensure This is Diabetic-Friendly & Family-Approved?

✓ Low-GI Ingredients Only – Little millet, moong dal, and coconut milk stabilise blood sugar.

✓ No Sugar Spikes – Natural sweeteners like dates or monk fruit provide subtle sweetness.

✓ Rich Flavour Without Sugar – Cardamom, saffron, coconut, and nuts make it delicious for everyone!

Serving Suggestions

Enjoy warm or chilled—pairs beautifully with a cup of unsweetened herbal tea!

For a vegan version, replace ghee with coconut oil.

"Skipping sweets entirely?

That's like reading a book and skipping the last chapter—where's the fun in that?"

Smart Cooking for Diabetes: 6 Essential Swaps & Millet Cooking Tips

Living with diabetes doesn't mean giving up on delicious food—it's all about making smart swaps and cooking mindfully. By choosing the right ingredients and techniques, you can enjoy flavourful, nutritious meals without blood sugar spikes.

6 Smart Swaps for Every Diabetic to Stay Healthy

1. Choose Whole Grains Over Refined Ones
   - Swap: White rice & refined flour → Millets, whole wheat, quinoa, and oats
   - Why? These low-GI alternatives digest slowly, stabilising blood sugar.
2. Pick Natural Sweeteners Over Refined Sugar
   - Swap: Sugar, artificial sweeteners → Dates, monk fruit, stevia, or coconut sugar (in moderation)
   - Why? They provide sweetness without sudden insulin spikes.
3. Balance Your Plate with Protein & Fibre
   - Swap: High-carb meals → Add lentils, nuts, seeds, paneer, eggs, or tofu
   - Why? Protein + Fibre = Slower digestion, preventing sugar fluctuations.
4. Use Healthy Fats Instead of Refined Oils
   - Swap: Vegetable & hydrogenated oils → Cold-pressed oils, ghee, coconut oil, and nuts
   - Why? They improve insulin sensitivity and heart health.
5. Mind Your Portions & Meal Timing
   - Swap: Oversized meals → Small, frequent meals with controlled portions
   - Why? Large meals lead to glucose spikes, while controlled portions maintain balance.
6. Stay Hydrated & Ditch Sugary Drinks
   - Swap: Packaged juices & sodas → Herbal teas, infused water, buttermilk
   - Why? Hydration supports metabolism and prevents cravings.

Stepping into the World of Millets – A Diabetic's Journey to Better Health

You've heard about **millets**, seen them at the grocery store, and maybe even read about their **low glycaemic index and health benefits**. But let's be honest—**where do you even start?**

If you're **diabetic or prediabetic**, you might feel a mix of **apprehension and excitement**.

Will millets really help control my blood sugar?

Will they taste good? Will my family enjoy them too?

What if I mess up the portions?

You're not alone!

What to Expect When You Start Cooking with Millets?

- ☑ **Your Blood Sugar May Stabilise** – But you need to track it! Everyone reacts differently, so **monitor your glucose levels** after meals.
- ☑ **Your Digestion May Improve** – The high fibre in millets can improve **gut health and regularity**.
- ☑ **You Might Feel Fuller Longer** – Unlike refined carbs, millets provide **sustained energy** without crashes.
- ☑ **Taste & Texture? It Grows on You!** – If you're used to white rice and wheat, millets may feel different at first. **Give your taste buds time to adjust.**

Every new change comes with questions, and that's perfectly okay. But here's the good news: You don't have to figure it all out at once.

Your Challenge: Try Millets for One Day!

Take this **one-day meal plan** and try it.

Track your sugar levels before and after meals.

Note how you **feel—energy, hunger levels, digestion.**

This is **your journey**.

You don't have to be perfect—you just have to **start**. **Are you ready?**

Start small. Experiment. Track your sugar levels.

8 Evidence-Based Diet Tips for Diabetics

1. **Maintain Consistent Meal Timing (Avoid Long Gaps)**
   - **Evidence:** Studies show that **irregular meal timing** can cause **blood sugar fluctuations and insulin resistance**.
   - **What to Do?** Eat **small, balanced meals every 3-4 hours** to maintain **steady glucose levels** and avoid sugar spikes.
2. **Stay Hydrated (Water is Your Best Friend!)**
   - **Evidence:** Dehydration **raises blood sugar levels** by making the blood more concentrated. The **American Diabetes Association (ADA)** recommends **adequate hydration** to support **glucose metabolism**.
   - **What to Do?** Aim for **2-3 litres of water daily**, including **herbal teas or infused water**. Avoid **sugary or carbonated drinks**.
3. **Ensure a Balanced Plate at Every Meal**
   - **Evidence:** The **Diabetes Plate Method** (ADA) suggests **½ plate non-starchy vegetables, ¼ plate protein, and ¼ plate whole grains or millets** to **stabilise post-meal sugar levels**.
   - **What to Do?** Every meal should have a **protein source (dal, paneer, tofu, nuts), healthy fats (ghee, coconut, seeds), and fibre (veggies, millets)** for **better insulin response**.
4. **Eat in the Right Order – Start with Fibre & Protein First**
   - **Evidence:** Studies published in the **Diabetes Care Journal** suggest that eating **fibre and protein before carbohydrates** helps **slow glucose absorption and reduce post-meal sugar spikes**.
   - **What to Do?** Start meals with **vegetables (fibre)** and **protein sources (dal, paneer, tofu, eggs)** before consuming **carbohydrates (millets, whole grains)**. This **lowers the glycaemic impact** and keeps insulin levels stable.

5. **Walk for 10-15 Minutes After Meals to Lower Blood Sugar**
   - **Evidence:** Research from the **American Diabetes Association** shows that **walking for 10-15 minutes post-meal** can **reduce blood sugar levels by 20-30%** compared to sitting. This is because movement helps **muscles use glucose efficiently**.
   - **What to Do?** After meals, take a **light walk** instead of sitting or lying down. Even **household activities** like folding laundry or washing dishes **help glucose regulation**.
6. Focus on Low Glycaemic Index (GI) Foods
   - **Evidence:** Studies published in the **American Journal of Clinical Nutrition** show that **low-GI foods** (GI < 55) help **prevent blood sugar spikes and improve insulin sensitivity**.
   - **What to Do?** Choose **millets, whole grains, legumes, nuts, and non-starchy vegetables** instead of high-GI refined carbs like white rice, bread, and sugary foods.
7. **HbA1c Test – The Long-Term Blood Sugar Check**
   - **Why It's Important:** Measures **average blood sugar over 2-3 months**, showing how well diabetes is managed.
   - **Target Range:**
     - **Below 5.7%** – Normal
     - **5.7% – 6.4%** – Prediabetes
     - **6.5% or Higher** – Diabetes
   - **How Often?** Every **3-6 months**.
8. **Fasting & Post-Meal Blood Sugar – Daily Monitoring**
   - **Why It's Important:** Helps track **real-time glucose levels** and adjust **diet & medication** accordingly.
   - **Target Range:**
     - **Fasting (before breakfast): 70-99 mg/dL (normal), 100-125 mg/dL (prediabetic), 126+ mg/dL (diabetic)**
     - **Post-meal (2 hours after eating): Below 140 mg/dL (normal), 140-199 mg/dL (prediabetic), 200+ mg/dL (diabetic)**
   - **How Often? Daily or weekly**, based on personal blood sugar trend

Diabetes Lifestyle Checklist

Daily Habits for Better Blood Sugar Control ☑

MEAL TIMING & FOOD ORDER

☑ Eat Every 3-4 Hours – Avoid long gaps to prevent sugar crashes or spikes.

☑ Start Meals with Fibre & Protein First – Eat vegetables & protein before carbs to slow glucose absorption.

☑ Choose Low-GI Carbs – Opt for millets, quinoa, whole grains, and legumes over refined carbs.

BALANCED PLATE METHOD

☑ ½ Plate Non-Starchy Vegetables – Leafy greens, bell peppers, okra, gourds, etc.

☑ ¼ Plate Protein – Lentils, paneer, eggs, chicken, tofu, or nuts.

☑ ¼ Plate Whole Grains or Millets – Ragi, bajra, foxtail millet, jowar.

☑ Healthy Fats in Moderation – Ghee, coconut, nuts, seeds, olive oil.

HYDRATION & SMART DRINKING CHOICES

☑ Drink 2-3 Litres of Water Daily – Dehydration raises blood sugar.

☑ Replace Sugary Drinks with Herbal Teas, Coconut Water, or Buttermilk.

☑ Limit Caffeine & Alcohol – Excess coffee or alcohol can disrupt insulin sensitivity.

PHYSICAL ACTIVITY & MOVEMENT

☑ Walk for 10-15 Minutes After Meals – Helps muscles use glucose efficiently.

☑ Do Strength Training 2-3 Times a Week – Builds muscle, improves insulin sensitivity.

☑ Get 7,000-10,000 Steps Daily – Even light activity helps regulate blood sugar.

SLEEP & STRESS MANAGEMENT

☑ Aim for 7-8 Hours of Quality Sleep – Poor sleep increases insulin resistance.

☑ Manage Stress with Meditation or Deep Breathing – Cortisol (stress hormone) spikes blood sugar.

☑ Avoid Late-Night Snacking – Helps maintain fasting glucose levels.

TRACKING & MONITORING

☑ Monitor Blood Sugar Before & After Meals – Helps identify food triggers.

☑ Rotate Millets & Whole Grains – Test how different millets affect your sugar levels.

☑ Keep a Food & Lifestyle Journal – Noting meals, exercise, and sugar readings helps find patterns.

💡 FINAL TIP: Small Changes → Big Results!

3-Day Diabetes-Friendly Sample Meal Plans

(Balanced, Protein-Rich & Low-GI)

Each day is designed to **stabilize blood sugar levels**, provide **adequate protein**, and ensure a **nutrient-dense, satisfying meal plan**.

These include **millets, healthy fats, low-GI fruits, nuts, seeds, and well-balanced macronutrients** while keeping an **eye on carbs**.

DAY 1 – South Indian Vegetarian (Millet & Plant-Based Protein Focus)

Early Morning Drink (6:30 AM)

☑ **Methi (Fenugreek) Water** – Soak 1 tsp methi seeds overnight and drink on an empty stomach.

Breakfast (8:00 AM)

☑ **Foxtail Millet Upma** (with sprouted moong, coconut, and ghee tempering)

☑ **A glass of spiced buttermilk** (jeera, ginger, curry leaves)

Mid-Morning Snack (10:30 AM)

☑ **A handful of soaked almonds & walnuts**

☑ **1 small bowl of diced guava (Low-GI fruit)**

Lunch (1:00 PM)

☑ **Bajra Roti (Pearl Millet Flatbread)**

☑ **Protein-Packed Sambar** (with dal, drumsticks, and pumpkin)

☑ **Steamed Green Beans Stir-Fry (Coconut & Curry Leaves)**

☑ **A bowl of fresh homemade yogurt**

Evening Snack (4:30 PM)

☑ **Turmeric & Cinnamon Tea** (No sugar)

☑ **Ragi & Flaxseed Laddu (Sweetened with dates paste)**

Dinner (7:30 PM)

☑ **Little Millet Pongal** (with moong dal & pepper)

☑ **Spinach & Methi Stir-Fry**

☑ **A glass of warm almond milk with a pinch of nutmeg**

DAY 2 – North Indian Vegetarian (High-Protein, Low-Carb, Millet-Based)

Early Morning Drink (6:30 AM)

☑ **Cinnamon Water** (Boil cinnamon sticks in water & drink warm)

Breakfast (8:00 AM)

☑ **Besan Chilla (Gram Flour Pancake) with Flaxseeds**

☑ **Mint & Cucumber Chutney**

☑ **A glass of spiced buttermilk**

Mid-Morning Snack (10:30 AM)

☑ **Pumpkin Seeds & Chia Seed Mix**

☑ **A small bowl of diced berries (strawberries & blueberries – Low-GI)**

Lunch (1:00 PM)

☑ **Foxtail millet vegetable pulao**

☑ **Methi & Paneer Bhurji** (Fenugreek + Scrambled Paneer)

☑ **Mixed Veg Raita (Cucumber, Tomato, & Jeera Yogurt)**

☑ **Sprouted Moong Dal Salad with Lemon Dressing**

Evening Snack (4:30 PM)

☑ **Sugar-Free Ragi Muffin**

☑ **Herbal Ginger Tea**

Dinner (7:30 PM)

☑ **Little millet Khichdi** (With moong dal, carrots & spinach)

☑ **A small bowl of Kadhi (Curd-based, low-carb dish)**

☑ **A handful of roasted makhana (fox nuts) for crunch**

DAY 3 – South Indian Non-Vegetarian (Lean Proteins + Millets + Low-GI Foods)

Early Morning Drink (6:30 AM)

☑ **Tulsi & Lemon Detox Water**

Breakfast (8:00 AM)

☑ **Egg & Ragi Dosa** (Ragi dosa topped with a sunny-side-up egg)

☑ **Coconut Chutney**

Mid-Morning Snack (10:30 AM)

☑ **A handful of mixed nuts (Almonds, Walnuts, Pumpkin Seeds)**

☑ **1 small apple (Low-GI fruit, high in fibre)**

Lunch (1:00 PM)

☑ **Ragi mudde/Littlefinger millet ball**

☑ **Grilled Chicken Curry (Low-oil, coconut-based, high protein)**

☑ **Stir-Fried Beans, carrot, cauliflower & Bell Peppers (Olive oil & garlic seasoning)**

☑ **A bowl of homemade yogurt**

Evening Snack (4:30 PM)

☑ **A glass of coconut water with 1 teaspoon of soaked chia seeds**

☑ **Ragi Crackers with Hummus Dip**

Dinner (7:30 PM)

☑ **Foxtail Millet & Chicken Soup** (Hearty, protein-rich)

☑ **Sautéed Mushrooms & Methi Stir-Fry**

☑ **Warm Haldi Doodh (Turmeric Almond Milk) before bed**

Key Takeaways for Diabetics from This Meal Plan

- ☑ **Balance Carbs with Protein & Fibre** – Every meal includes **a protein source + millets/whole grains + non-starchy vegetables** to **prevent sugar spikes.**
- ☑ **Hydration is Key** – Each day starts with a **blood sugar-regulating morning drink** and encourages **2-3 litres of water**.
- ☑ **Low-GI Fruits Only** – Guava, berries, apple – No high-GI fruits like mango, banana
- ☑ **Healthy Fats for Insulin Sensitivity** – Ghee, coconut, olive oil, nuts, and seeds are included in moderation.
- ☑ **Evening Walks Post-Dinner** – A **10-15 min walk** is recommended after meals to **regulate glucose levels**

SUCCESS STORY – 3

Arathi's Journey: From Fear to Freedom – A Decade Without Diabetes

---

When Arathi, a 46-year-old woman, walked into AlaMirap Nutrition, she was scared, frustrated, and overwhelmed.

Her doctor had just told her she was prediabetic.

❌ "I don't want to start medication."

❌ "I never thought this would happen to me. I've always been careful… haven't I?"

❌ "What if I can't reverse it? What if it turns into full-blown diabetes?"

That fear gripped her heart, but something inside her refused to give up.

She was ready for change.

The Turning Point: Finding a Way Out

Arathi didn't just want a quick fix—she wanted a real solution.

At Alamirap, we listened to her fears, her struggles, and her hopes. Instead of handing her a generic diet plan, we gave her a tool to understand her body—Continuous Glucose Monitoring (CGM).

For the first time in her life, she saw exactly how food affected her blood sugar.

It was eye-opening.

💡 The "healthy" breakfast she thought was good for her was actually spiking her sugars.

💡 A simple tweak—starting her meals with fibre & protein—made a huge difference.

💡 She didn't have to eat less—she had to eat smarter.

We introduced her to our GLAM Diet (Glucose Level Assisted Monitoring Diet), designed to work with her metabolism, not against it.

- ✓ Glycaemic Load Control – Balanced, whole-food meals with low-GI, high-fibre choices.
- ✓ Lifestyle Optimisation – A focus on movement, hydration, and sleep.
- ✓ Active Monitoring – Using CGM data to create a personalised nutrition plan.
- ✓ Mindful Eating – Understanding meal timing, portion control, and carb-protein balance.

Her First Steps: Small Changes, Big Wins

In the beginning, it wasn't easy. Her sugar cravings were strong. Her energy levels were unpredictable. Her fear of diabetes was still there. But week by week, something changed.

☑ She started working out at home—just small stretches and walks.

☑ Her sugar spikes reduced.

☑ Her body felt lighter, her mind clearer.

A month later, she took a leap.

She joined a yoga class. And that changed everything. She felt stronger, more in control, and for the first time in years, she felt free from fear.

Three Months Later: A New Arathi Emerges

She walked into our clinic, smiling. "I just got my latest blood test results. My sugar levels have dropped!" Her HbA1c had improved. Her energy was steady.

Her weight had come down—without starving herself.

She had reversed her prediabetes and she had done it without medication.

A Decade Later: More Than Just One Woman's Story

Today, Arathi is 56 years old. She is STILL diabetes-free. Her entire family eats better, moves more, and lives healthier. She has inspired her friends to start their own journeys.

What started as one woman's fear turned into a ripple effect that changed lives.

"If I Can Do It, Anyone Can." – Arathi's Message to You

"I thought diabetes was inevitable. It wasn't."

"I didn't need extreme diets—I needed balance, science, and the right guidance."

"I didn't just change my food—I changed my mindset, my habits, my life."

If you're struggling with prediabetes or diabetes, you don't have to do it alone.

You CAN take control of your health with diet, lifestyle modifications

You CAN eat delicious, wholesome meals—without fear of sugar spikes.

You CAN build a lifestyle that works for YOU – just do it Scientifically.

Take the first step today. Let's reverse diabetes, together.

SUCCESS STORY - 4

A Love That Stood the Test of Time: How a 60-Year Marriage & the Right Nutrition Led to a Diabetes-Free Life

Some love stories are written in grand gestures. Some are built in the **quiet strength of companionship.** And some, like this one, are about **fighting for each other's health, happiness, and freedom—one meal at a time.**

This is the story of an **80-year-old husband Vikram and his 75-year-old wife Rani**, who have been together for **60 years—six decades of love, care, and unwavering devotion.**

She had **only one wish. "I want to see my husband free from insulin."**

A Wife's Hope, A Husband's Journey

Despite living with **Type 2 diabetes for 40 years**, her husband had always been **extremely disciplined with his diet**. He followed **doctor's advice, exercised lightly, and made careful food choices.** Yet, he remained dependent on **8 units of insulin every night**. He was okay but his **wife's heart wasn't at peace. She wished to see him free from injections.**

Then one day, she saw **my program on Zee TV** "Oggranne Dabbi" where I was talking about my journey of optimal blood sugar controls in spite of being a diabetic since 1994. Something **clicked inside her**. She turned to him and said, **"Let's try this together."**

Parimala is walking in the shoes of a diabetic since decades. She can feel us.

And just like that, with a **heart full of hope**, they walked into **Alamirap Nutrition**, ready to make a change—**together.**

Millets, Mindful Eating & The GLAM Diet: A Gentle, Science-Backed Approach

We knew one thing—at 80 years old, his body needed time to adjust.

We didn't **drastically change** his food. Instead, we introduced **The GLAM Diet (Glucose Level Assisted Monitoring Diet)**—a structured, **science-backed** plan that **allowed his body to adapt naturally.**

We sat with the couple and made detailed notes of their regular dietary choices. We worked with his wife, what are the simple swaps we could start with so that we don't burden his digestion.

✓ Glycaemic Load Control – Instead of eliminating carbs, we balanced them **with protein and fibre**.

✓ Lifestyle Optimisation – A focus on **hydration, movement, and stress-free eating habits**.

✓ Active Monitoring – His **blood sugar was tracked daily**, so we knew what was working.

✓ Mindful Eating – Slowly **swapping refined grains with gut-friendly millets**, without shocking his system.

Introducing Millets: A Gentle Transition, A Lasting Impact

Due to his **age and sensitive digestion**, we knew that introducing millets had to be **gradual and mindful**.

- **Week 1:** We swapped **one meal a day**—instead of rice, he had soft **millet khichdi**
- **Week 2:** We introduced soft **bajra roti** in place of wheat chapati for easy digestion.
- **Week 3:** We added **foxtail millet dosa**, a gentle yet nutritious alternative.

All the while, **his body adjusted beautifully**. There was **no discomfort, no bloating, no upset stomach.** And then, something **amazing happened.**

The Gradual Insulin Reduction: A Dream Becoming Reality

- **After just two weeks**, his **doctor reduced his insulin from 8 units to 4 units.**
- **After a month**, his blood sugar readings remained **steady and controlled.**
- **At the end of the second month, his doctor made the decision—"No more insulin."**
- **And for the first time in 40 years, his nights were free from insulin injections.**

A Wife's Love, A Heartwarming Moment

The day his **doctor officially stopped his insulin**, his **wife held his hands, looked at us, and her eyes welled up with tears. "This is the happiest I've been in years. You've given him freedom. And you've given me peace."**

A Love Story That Inspires Us All

Today, at 80, this gentleman lives without insulin. His wife, his biggest cheerleader, makes sure every meal is filled with love and balance. Their story is a reminder that love isn't just about romance—it's about showing up for each other, every single day.

> **"Age is just a number. It is never too late to reverse your way back to Wellness"**

If We Could Do It, So Can You.

SUCCESS STORY - 5

Little Warrior: The Heartbreaking Yet Inspiring Story of an 8-Year-Old with Type 1 Diabetes

Most eight-year-olds dream of birthday cakes, running wild in the park, and sharing chocolates with friends. But for **Aryan**, life was different. There were **no chocolates. No carefree meals. No skipping dinner just because he didn't feel like eating.**

Instead, there were **finger pricks, insulin shots, and constant calculations of food and sugar levels.** And the hardest part? **He had no parents to hold him through it all.**

A Child's Battle

Aryan's world **shattered** when he was just **four years old**. A tragic **car accident** took both his parents away. His grandparents—two elderly souls who had already lived their share of struggles—**became his entire world.** They were **grieving, yet they held him.** They were **aging, yet they learned.** They were **scared, yet they stayed strong—for him.** Just as Aryan was starting to understand his loss, another cruel twist awaited him. At age **six,** he was diagnosed with **Type 1 diabetes**.

For the second time in his short life, **his world turned upside down.**

An 8-Year-Old's Daily Routine That Would Break Most Adults

Unlike Type 2 diabetes, **Type 1 is not caused by diet or lifestyle**—it's an autoimmune condition. That meant Aryan would **never grow out of it.** That meant:

Insulin injections every single day. Finger pricks multiple times a day. Strict meal planning—no sweets, no indulgences, no "I don't want to eat today."

And yet, this **tiny warrior never complained.**

He learned to count carbs before he even knew long division.

He watched his food, not with frustration, but with understanding.

He adapted, not because he wanted to, but because he had to.

His grandparents often cried **when he wasn't looking**. Not because they were tired. Not because they felt burdened. But because **no child should have to live like this.**

Because **they wished they could take his pain away.** Because **all they wanted was to see him live a normal life.**

The Hardest Challenge: A Child Without Sweets

One evening, as Aryan sat at the dining table, his grandmother noticed him staring at a **chocolate wrapper** in his hand. It was from a birthday party at school. She saw the **wistfulness in his eyes.** The longing of a child who just wanted to be like everyone else. She braced herself for the inevitable question.

"Can I have it, Ajji?"

She swallowed the lump in her throat. She had told him **"no"** so many times before.

But this time, before she could answer, **Aryan did something that broke her heart yet filled it with pride. He slowly folded the wrapper, put it in his pocket, and smiled.**

"It's okay. I just wanted to keep it. It smells nice."

That night, his grandmother cried herself to sleep.

Her **eight-year-old grandson had already learned self-control beyond his years.**

A Ray of Hope: Giving Aryan the Freedom to Enjoy Life Again

Aryan's grandparents searched for ways to **give him a childhood he deserved.**

That's when they found **Alamirap Nutrition**. They learned about the **GLAM Diet**, a way to **balance his blood sugar naturally** while still allowing him **the joy of food.**

We worked closely with Aryan, creating a **Type 1-friendly meal plan** that:

✓ **Used low-GI ingredients** like millets, nuts, and fiber-rich foods to keep sugar stable.

✓ **Introduced sugar-free, healthy alternatives** for his favorite sweets.

✓ **Monitored his response through Continuous Glucose Monitoring (CGM)** to personalize his diet.

For the first time in years, **Aryan got to enjoy a dessert made just for him—a sugar-free ragi and almond ladoo.**

His eyes lit up. **"This tastes like real sweets, Ajji!"** His grandmother wiped a tear and smiled. **"That's because it is, muddhu (dear). And you deserve it."**

A Future Full of Possibilities

Aryan wants to become a diabetologist and help other kids like him when he grows up. He no longer feels like he's missing out—because now, he knows he can still enjoy life, just in a different way.

Challenges Faced by a Type 1 Diabetic

Living with **Type 1 diabetes** is a **constant balancing act**—between food, insulin, physical activity, and emotional well-being. Unlike Type 2 diabetes, which can be managed with lifestyle changes, **Type 1 diabetics require lifelong insulin therapy**, making **diet, exercise, and mental resilience critical.**

3 Major Nutrition Challenges

1. **Carb Counting & Blood Sugar Spikes**
   - Every meal must be carefully planned to **balance carbohydrates, proteins, and fats**.
   - **Even healthy foods can cause unexpected sugar spikes.**
2. **Restriction from Sweets & Processed Foods**
   - **Chocolates, desserts, and packaged foods** are difficult to manage due to **hidden sugars and high-GI ingredients**.
   - This can lead to **feelings of deprivation, especially in children.**
3. **Timing & Consistency in Meals**
   - Skipping meals or **eating at irregular times** can **disrupt blood sugar control**.
   - Unlike others who can eat spontaneously, **Type 1 diabetics need to eat on a schedule to align with insulin doses.**

     - **1 Physical Activity Challenge**
4. **Exercise Can Be a Double-Edged Sword**
   - Physical activity **lowers blood sugar**, but **overexertion without proper planning can cause dangerous hypoglycemia (low blood sugar)**.
   - They need to **eat strategically before and after workouts** to prevent sudden crashes.

     - **1 Emotional Challenge**
5. **The Mental Burden of Always "Being Careful"**
   - **Endless monitoring, finger pricks, insulin shots, and meal restrictions** create **an emotional toll**, leading to **frustration, anxiety, or burnout**.
   - Many feel **left out in social situations** or **overwhelmed by constant vigilance**.

How Millets Can Help Type 1 Diabetics

Millets are **low-GI, fibre-rich, and slow-digesting grains** that can make life **easier and healthier** for Type 1 diabetics.

1. **Steady Blood Sugar Levels**
   - Unlike rice and wheat, **millets digest slowly**, preventing sudden spikes and crashes in blood sugar.
2. **Better Satiety & Reduced Hunger Cravings**
   - Millets are **high in fibre** and **keep you full longer**, reducing the **urge for unhealthy snacks.**
3. **Naturally Gluten-Free & Gut-Friendly**
   - Many Type 1 diabetics struggle with **gut issues**. Millets are easy on digestion and **improve gut health.**
4. **Nutritious & Versatile for Balanced Meals**
   - Can be used in **porridges, rotis, dosas, khichdi, and desserts,** making them **a great alternative to high-GI grains.**
5. **Reduces Insulin Resistance Over Time**
   - Regular millet consumption **improves insulin sensitivity**, making it **easier to manage daily sugar levels.**

Type 1 diabetes is a lifelong journey, but the right food choices—like millets—can make it smoother, healthier, and make you feel more in control of the situation.

A Final Thought: The Strength of a Child, The Love of a Family

In our busy lives, we often **take things for granted**—sweets, meals, health. But children like Aryan remind us that some battles are fought **in silence, with bravery beyond their years.**

If you or your loved one is struggling with Type 1 diabetes, know this: It is possible to live a full, happy, and healthy life.

With the right nutrition, guidance, and a bit of love, even the smallest warriors can win the biggest battles.

Chapter 5

GUT HEALTH & ANTI-INFLAMMATORY DIETS – THE BUZZWORDS SHAPING HEALTH & WEIGHT LOSS TRENDS

What is Gut Health & Why Does It Matter?

Your gut is home to **trillions of bacteria** (good & bad), collectively called the **gut microbiome**. When balanced, they help with:

☑ **Better Digestion** – Absorbing nutrients efficiently & reducing bloating.

☑ **Weight Regulation** – A healthy gut supports **fat metabolism & appetite control**.

☑ **Stronger Immunity** – 70% of your immune system **resides in the gut**.

☑ **Mental Health Connection** – Gut health affects **mood, anxiety & stress levels** (the **gut-brain axis**).

The Anti-Inflammatory Diet – The Game Changer for Weight Loss & Gut Healing

Chronic **inflammation is the hidden culprit** behind obesity, diabetes, and gut disorders. The **Anti-Inflammatory Diet** focuses on:

- **Whole, Unprocessed Foods** – Millets, vegetables, healthy fats, and lean proteins.
- **Cutting Out Triggers** – Processed sugar, refined oils, excessive dairy, and artificial additives.
- **Balancing Omega-3 & Omega-6 Fats** – More **avocados, nuts, ghee**, less processed seed oils.

From **celebrities to fitness experts**, everyone is talking about **gut health and inflammation**—and for good reason! Whether it's **weight loss, diabetes control, or overall well-being**, science now confirms that **a healthy gut is key to long-term health**.

So why has **gut health become the hottest wellness trend?**

- **Celebrity Transformations** – Big names are crediting **gut-healing diets** for weight loss, better digestion, and glowing skin.
- **Scientific Backing** – Research links **gut microbiome balance** with **metabolism, immunity, and mental health**.
- **The "Food as Medicine" Shift** – People are realizing that **fixing the gut can fix many chronic health issues**.

5 Foods That Celebrities Swear By for Gut Health & Inflammation Control

1. **Fermented Foods** – Kombucha, homemade curd, kanji, kimchi (Probiotic-rich = Gut-friendly).
2. **Leafy Greens & Colourful Veggies** – Spinach, beets, and turmeric (Packed with antioxidants).
3. **Millets Over Refined Grains** – Ragi, foxtail millet, bajra (Rich in fibre, feeds good gut bacteria).
4. **Healthy Fats** – Ghee, coconut, olive oil, nuts (Fights inflammation).
5. **Bone Broth & Collagen-Rich Foods** – Strengthens gut lining & improves digestion.

How to Start an Anti-Inflammatory, Gut-Healing Diet Today?

☑ **Eat More Fibre** – Include **millets, flaxseeds, and fresh vegetables** in every meal.

☑ **Reduce Sugar & Processed Foods** – Swap **sugar with dates or stevia, and opt for whole foods**.

☑ **Hydrate with Herbal Teas & Infused Water** – Tulsi, ginger, turmeric teas help **reduce inflammation**.

☑ **Include Probiotics & Prebiotics** – Eat **homemade curd, kanji, or fermented veggies** daily.

☑ **Track Your Gut's Reaction to Foods** – Observe bloating, energy levels, and digestion after meals.

Did You Know? *Fascinating Facts About Gut Health!*

1. **Your Gut is Your Second Brain!**
   - The gut has **over 100 million neurons**, producing **90% of your body's serotonin**—the "happiness hormone." This is why **gut health directly affects mood, stress, and even anxiety levels!**
2. **You Have More Bacteria Than Human Cells!**
   - The gut microbiome is home to **trillions of bacteria**, outnumbering human cells **10 to 1**. A balanced gut microbiome **boosts immunity, improves digestion, and even helps with weight loss**.

3. **70% of Your Immune System Lives in Your Gut!**
   - A healthy gut microbiome **defends against infections, reduces inflammation, and prevents autoimmune diseases**. That's why **healing your gut = strengthening your immunity**!

Top Indian Gut-Healing Foods & Their Benefits

A strong gut microbiome means **better digestion, immunity, and metabolism**.

Here's a **list of powerful gut-healing foods** that should be a part of your diet:

1. **Fermented Foods – Rich in Probiotics (Good Gut Bacteria)**
   - ☑ **Homemade Curd (Dahi)** – Contains **Lactobacillus** that promotes **healthy gut flora**.
   - ☑ **Buttermilk (Chaas)** – Probiotic drink that aids **digestion & prevents acidity**.
   - ☑ **Kanji (Fermented Beet/Carrot Water)** – Fermented with **mustard seeds**, it's loaded with **good bacteria & antioxidants**.
   - ☑ **Idli & Dosa Batter** – Naturally fermented, improves **gut-friendly bacterial diversity**.
2. **Prebiotic-Rich Foods – Feed the Good Gut Bacteria**
   - ☑ **Banana Stem & Raw Banana** – High in **resistant starch**, supports digestion & relieves bloating.
   - ☑ **Garlic & Onion** – Rich in **prebiotics** that help **good bacteria multiply**.
   - ☑ **Sprouted Moong Dal & Lentils** – Boosts **enzyme production & gut-friendly fibre**.
   - ☑ **Jackfruit Flour** – A natural **gut cleanser** that helps in **bowel regulation**.

3. **Millet-Based Foods – Gluten-Free & Easy on Digestion**
   - ☑ **Foxtail Millet (Thinai)** – Loaded with **soluble fibre**, great for digestion & gut healing.
   - ☑ **Ragi (Finger Millet)** – High in **prebiotic fibre**, supports gut microbiome balance.
   - ☑ **Bajra (Pearl Millet)** – Reduces **gut inflammation & acidity**.
   - ☑ **Little Millet (Saamai)** – Light on digestion, helps with **gut motility**.
4. **Herbal Teas & Spices – Natural Digestive Boosters**
   - ☑ **Ajwain (Carom Seeds) Water** – Soothes bloating & indigestion.
   - ☑ **Saunf (Fennel) Tea** – A natural coolant, prevents **acidity & gut spasms**.
   - ☑ **Ginger & Turmeric Tea** – **Anti-inflammatory**, helps heal the **gut lining**.
   - ☑ **Cumin Water (Jeera Pani)** – Stimulates **enzyme production & digestion**.
5. **Gut-Healing Comfort Foods**
   - ☑ **Khichdi (Rice + Moong Dal)** – The ultimate **meal**, perfect for gut healing.
   - ☑ **Bone Broth** – Rich in **collagen & amino acids**, strengthens the gut lining.
   - ☑ **Warm Ghee Rice** – **Ghee contains butyrate**, which repairs the gut wall.
   - ☑ **Coconut & Curry Leaf Chutney** – Coconut has **healthy fats** that reduce gut inflammation.

Millets & Gut Health – The Evidence-Based Connection

Millets have gained **superfood status** in gut health. These **ancient grains** play a **critical role in maintaining a healthy gut microbiome.**

What Science Says About Millets & Gut Health

1. **Rich in Prebiotic Fibre – Feeds Good Gut Bacteria**
    - **Evidence:** A study published in the *Frontiers in Microbiology* journal shows that **prebiotics in whole grains like millets** promote the growth of **beneficial gut bacteria.**
    - **Why It Matters?** A healthy gut microbiome supports **digestion, immunity, and mental health.**
2. **Anti-Inflammatory & Easy to Digest**
    - **Evidence:** Research from *Nutrients Journal* highlights that **millets contain polyphenols and antioxidants** that **reduce gut inflammation.**
    - **Why It Matters?** Millets help **heal leaky gut**, reduce **IBS symptoms**, and promote better digestion.
3. **Gluten-Free & Gentle on the Stomach**
    - **Evidence:** Studies from the *American Journal of Gastroenterology* confirm that **gluten sensitivity can cause gut inflammation** and bloating.
    - **Why It Matters?** Since **millets are naturally gluten-free**, they are **safer for gut health** than refined wheat-based foods.
4. **Low Glycaemic Index (GI) – Prevents Gut Dysbiosis**
    - **Evidence:** Research in *Diabetes & Metabolism Journal* suggests that **high-GI foods trigger gut inflammation and disrupt microbiome balance.**
    - **Why It Matters? Millets help in balancing gut microbiome.**

5. **Packed with Resistant Starch - Supports Gut Lining**
   - **Evidence:** According to *The British Journal of Nutrition*, **resistant starch in millets** acts as a **natural gut healer**, reducing acidity and promoting the production of **short-chain fatty acids (SCFAs)**.
   - **Why It Matters?** SCFAs strengthen **intestinal walls**, improve **nutrient absorption**, and reduce **gut-related disorders**.

Best Millets for Gut Health & How to Use Them

- **Foxtail Millet** - High in **soluble fibre**, great for digestion. *(Use in upma, porridge, dosas.)*
- **Ragi (Finger Millet)** - Rich in **calcium & prebiotics**, strengthens gut health. *(Use in porridges, idlis, or rotis.)*
- **Bajra (Pearl Millet)** - Anti-inflammatory, good for gut healing. *(Use in rotis, khichdi, or soups.)*
- **Little Millet** - Light on digestion, prevents bloating. *(Use in payasam, pulao, or stir-fries.)*

How to Include Millets in a Gut-Healing Diet

☑ **Start Slow & Rotate Millets** - Introduce 1 millet at a time and observe digestion.

☑ **Pair with Probiotics** - Eat with **curd, kanji, or fermented pickles** for maximum gut benefits.

☑ **Cook with Ghee & Spices** - Adding **turmeric, ginger, and black pepper** enhances digestion.

☑ **Avoid Overprocessing** - Stick to **whole millets over millet flours** for better fibre content.

What is a Probiotic and what is its role in Gut health?

Probiotics are live beneficial bacteria that support gut health, digestion, and immunity. They help maintain a healthy balance of gut microbiota, improving **nutrient absorption, reducing inflammation, and enhancing overall well-being.**

7 Examples of Probiotic Foods:

1. **Homemade Curd (Dahi)** – Rich in **Lactobacillus** bacteria, aids digestion.
2. **Buttermilk (Chaas)** – A cooling probiotic drink that reduces acidity.
3. **Kanji (Fermented Carrot/Beetroot Drink)** – Boosts gut-friendly bacteria & immunity.
4. **Idli & Dosa Batter** – Naturally fermented, supports gut microbiome.
5. **Sauerkraut/Kimchi (Fermented Cabbage)** – High in probiotics & antioxidants.
6. **Kombucha (Fermented Tea)** – A refreshing probiotic detox drink.
7. **Fermented Pickles (Without Vinegar)** – Enhances digestion & provides good bacteria.

   Let's START with a very simple Millet Recipe for GUT Health

Recipe 20 – Ragi Ambali (Fermented Finger Millet Drink)

A Gut-Friendly, Diabetes-Friendly Super Drink!

Ragi Ambali is a **traditional South Indian probiotic drink**, packed with **gut-healing properties, prebiotic fibre, and essential minerals**. It is a **cooling, refreshing**, and **highly nutritious** beverage that helps in **blood sugar control, digestion, and hydration**.

Ingredients (Serves 2-3)

- ¼ cup ragi (finger millet) flour
- 2 cups water
- ½ cup buttermilk (or curd + water, whisked well)
- ½ tsp cumin powder (jeera powder)
- A pinch of salt
- A few curry leaves (optional, finely chopped)
- A small piece of ginger (grated, optional)
- Coriander leaves (for garnish, optional)

Step-by-Step Method

Step 1: Cook the Ragi Flour

1. In a pan, mix **ragi flour with 1 cup water**, ensuring there are no lumps.
2. Cook on **medium flame**, stirring continuously for **5-7 minutes** until the mixture thickens.
3. Add **1 more cup of water**, stir well, and let it cook for **2-3 more minutes**.
4. Turn off the flame and let it cool completely.

Step 2: Fermentation (Optional, But Highly Beneficial)

5. Once cooled, transfer the cooked ragi mix to a bowl and **let it ferment overnight (8-10 hours)**.
    - **Why Fermentation?** This enhances **probiotics, improves digestion, and makes it gut-friendly.**

Step 3: Prepare the Ambali Drink

6. Once fermented, mix the ragi with **buttermilk** (or whisked curd + water).
7. Add **salt, cumin powder, grated ginger, and finely chopped curry leaves.**
8. Stir well until smooth.

Step 4: Serve & Enjoy! Add Sattu powder for extra protein punch.

Best Food Pairings with Ragi Ambali for a Complete, Balanced Meal

Ragi Ambali is a **cooling, probiotic-rich drink**, but pairing it with the right foods can make it a **nutrient-dense, complete meal**. Here are **three food combinations** that balance **protein, fibre, and healthy fats** for better digestion, energy, and blood sugar control.

1. **Ragi Ambali + Sprout Salad**
   - **Why?** Sprouts are rich in **protein, fibre, and enzymes**, making them the perfect **gut-friendly and blood sugar-stabilizing** pair for Ambali.
   - **How to Prepare?**
     - Mix **sprouted moong, black chana, and peanuts.**
     - Add **grated carrots, cucumber, coriander, and lemon juice.**
     - Sprinkle with **rock salt and roasted jeera powder** for taste.

   ✓ **Benefits:** High in **digestive enzymes, plant-based protein & prebiotic fibre.**

2. **Ragi Ambali + Bajra Roti & Chutney**
   - **Why?** Bajra (pearl millet) is another **low-GI grain** that complements **ragi's calcium and fibre content.**
   - **How to Prepare?**
     - Make a **soft bajra roti** using warm water and ghee.
     - Pair with **coconut chutney** (coconut + green chilies + ginger + curry leaves).

✓ **Benefits:** Provides **slow-digesting carbs, good fats, and essential minerals**.

3. **Ragi Ambali + Steamed Vegetables & Dal**
   - **Why?** Steamed veggies provide **micronutrients**, while dal adds **protein and fibre**, making it a well-rounded meal.
   - **How to Prepare?**
     - Lightly steam **broccoli, carrots, beans, and pumpkin**.
     - Make a **simple moong dal** with cumin, garlic, and turmeric.
     - Serve with **a small bowl of Ambali** for a refreshing finish.

✓ **Benefits: Balances blood sugar, supports digestion, and provides complete nutrition**.

Recipe 21 – Little Millet Ganji (Light Digestive Porridge)

A Soothing & Nutritious Meal

Little Millet Ganji is a light, easily digestible, and gut-friendly porridge that is perfect for diabetics, those recovering from illness, and anyone looking for a comforting meal. It is naturally gluten-free, rich in fibre, and helps regulate blood sugar levels.

Ingredients (Serves 2-3)

- **¼ cup little millet (samai), washed & soaked for 30 minutes**
- **2 cups water**
- **½ cup buttermilk or whisked curd (for digestion & probiotics)**
- **½ tsp cumin powder (jeera powder, aids digestion)**
- **A pinch of rock salt**
- **A few curry leaves (optional, for flavour & gut health)**
- **1 tsp ghee (for healthy fats & absorption of nutrients)**
- **A handful of coriander leaves (for garnish, optional)**

Step-by-Step Preparation

Step 1: Cook the Little Millet

1. **In a pan, add little millet and 2 cups of water.**
2. **Cook on medium flame for 10-12 minutes, stirring occasionally.**
3. **Once the millet softens and the mixture thickens, turn off the heat.**

Step 2: Add Probiotics & Spices

4. **Let the cooked millet cool slightly before adding buttermilk or whisked curd.**
5. **Add cumin powder, salt, and curry leaves.**
6. **Stir well to combine all the ingredients.**

Step 3: Tempering & Serving

7. **In a small pan, heat 1 tsp ghee and add curry leaves or jeera (optional).**
8. **Pour the tempering over the ganji and mix gently.**
9. **Garnish with chopped coriander leaves and serve warm or at room temperature.**

How to Make Little Millet Ganji Protein-Rich?

Little Millet alone is a great source of fibre and minerals, but adding protein enhances its nutrition.

✅ 1. Add Sprouted Moong Dal 🌱

- Cook 2 tbsp sprouted moong dal along with the millet for extra plant-based protein & enzymes.

✅ 2. Mix in Almond or Peanut Powder 🥜

- Blend 1 tbsp roasted peanuts or almonds and mix it into the ganji for added protein & healthy fats.

✅ 3. Pair with a Side of Roasted Paneer or Boiled Eggs 🍳

- For a complete meal, serve the ganji with grilled paneer cubes or a boiled egg.

✅ 4. Use Sattu (Roasted Gram Flour) for an Extra Protein Boost 🥣

- Mix 1 tbsp sattu (roasted chana flour) with water and stir it into the ganji before serving.

3 Interesting Facts About Little Millet (Samai)

✅ **1. Low Glycaemic Index (GI) – Great for Blood Sugar Control**

- **Little Millet has a GI of ~52**, making it a **better choice than rice or wheat for diabetics**.
- It **releases glucose slowly**, preventing sudden sugar spikes.

☑ **2. High in Iron & Magnesium – Supports Energy & Heart Health**

- **Rich in iron**, which helps in **preventing anaemia**.
- **High magnesium content** supports **heart function and muscle relaxation**.

☑ **3. Best Swap for White Rice – More Fibre, More Nutrition**

- **Swap white rice** with little millet in **khichdi, pulao, upma, or porridge** for **higher fibre & better blood sugar control**.
- Cooks **faster than other millets**, making it an **easy and versatile grain** to use daily.

Recipe 22 – Pearl Millet Koozh (Fermented Bajra Porridge)

A Traditional Gut-Healing Drink

Pearl Millet Koozh, also known as **Bajra Koozh**, is a **fermented, probiotic-rich porridge** that has been consumed in India for centuries. It is known for its **cooling effect, gut-friendly properties, and ability to sustain energy levels for long periods**. This drink is perfect for **diabetics, weight management, and digestion**.

Ingredients (Serves 2-3)

- **½ cup pearl millet (bajra), washed & soaked overnight**
- **2 cups water**
- **½ cup buttermilk (or whisked curd + water for probiotic benefits)**
- **½ tsp cumin powder (jeera, aids digestion)**
- **A pinch of salt (rock salt preferred)**
- **A few curry leaves (optional, finely chopped for extra flavour & gut health)**
- **1 tsp ghee (for healthy fats & nutrient absorption, optional)**
- **A handful of coriander leaves (for garnish, optional)**

Step-by-Step Preparation

Step 1: Cook the Pearl Millet

1. Drain the **soaked pearl millet** and grind it into a coarse paste.
2. In a pan, add the **ground millet and 2 cups of water**.
3. Cook on **medium flame for 10-12 minutes**, stirring continuously to avoid lumps.
4. Once the mixture thickens, turn off the flame and **let it cool completely**.

Step 2: Fermentation (Essential for Probiotic Benefits)

5. Once cooled, transfer the cooked millet mixture to a bowl.
6. Cover and **let it ferment overnight (8-10 hours) at room temperature.**
   - **Why Fermentation?** This enhances **good gut bacteria, improves digestion, and increases bioavailability of nutrients.**

Step 3: Prepare the Koozh Drink

7. The next morning, mix the fermented millet paste with **buttermilk or whisked curd + water.**
8. Add **salt, cumin powder, and finely chopped curry leaves.**
9. Stir well to combine all ingredients until smooth.

Step 4: Tempering & Serving

10. In a small pan, heat **1 tsp ghee** (optional) and add **curry leaves or jeera** for a simple tempering.
11. Pour over the koozh, mix gently, and garnish with **chopped coriander leaves.**
12. Serve **chilled or at room temperature** for a refreshing, nourishing meal.

How to Make Pearl Millet Koozh Protein-Rich?

1. **Add Sprouted Moong Dal**
   - Cook **2 tbsp sprouted moong dal** with the millet for extra **plant-based protein & digestive enzymes.**
2. **Mix in Roasted Gram Powder (Sattu)**
   - Stir in **1 tbsp roasted gram flour (sattu)** for a **natural protein boost.**
3. **Serve with a Side of Boiled Eggs or Grilled Paneer**
   - A small **boiled egg** or **paneer cubes** will **increase the protein content and make it a complete meal.**
4. **Blend in Flaxseeds or Chia Seeds**
   - Adding **1 tsp flaxseeds or chia seeds** will provide **omega-3 fatty acids & additional protein.**

Did You Know? *3 Fascinating Facts About Pearl Millet (Bajra)* 🌾

☑ 1. Pearl Millet Has 8 Times More Iron Than Rice 🩸

- It is one of the richest plant-based sources of iron, making it great for anaemia prevention and energy production.

☑ 2. It Can Keep You Full for Hours & Aids Weight Loss 🍽

- Pearl millet is high in resistant starch & fibre, which slows digestion, prevents cravings, and supports gut health.

☑ 3. Naturally Gluten-Free & Alkaline – Great for Digestion 🦠

- Unlike wheat, bajra is easy on the stomach, reducing acidity, bloating, and inflammation, making it ideal for gut health & diabetes management.

Recipe 23 – Millet & Methi Gut-Cleansing Khichdi

Wholesome, light, and rich in fibre and prebiotics.

Ingredients:

- Little millet (saamai) – ½ cup
- Moong dal (split yellow lentils) – ¼ cup
- Fresh methi (fenugreek) leaves – ½ cup (chopped)
- Ginger – 1 tsp (grated)
- Garlic – 2 cloves (crushed)
- Cumin seeds (jeera) – 1 tsp
- Ajwain (carom seeds) – ½ tsp
- Turmeric powder – ¼ tsp
- Black pepper – ½ tsp (freshly crushed)
- Hing (asafoetida) – a pinch
- Rock salt or pink salt – to taste
- Water – 3 cups
- Ghee – 1 tbsp

Preparation

1. Wash & Soak
   - Rinse little millet and moong dal 2–3 times.
   - Soak together in water for 15–20 minutes (optional but helps digestion).
2. Sauté Spices & Aromatics
   - Heat ghee in a pressure cooker or heavy-bottomed pan.
   - Add cumin, ajwain, and a pinch of hing. Let them sizzle.
   - Add ginger and garlic. Sauté till aromatic.
3. Add Methi & Spices
   - Add chopped methi leaves and sauté for 2–3 minutes till slightly wilted.
   - Sprinkle turmeric, black pepper, and salt. Mix well.

4. Add Grains & Cook
    - Drain the soaked millet and dal. Add to the pan and mix well with the methi-spice base.
    - Pour in 3 cups of water. Stir everything together.
5. Cook Until Soft
    - If using a pressure cooker: cook on medium flame for 2–3 whistles.
    - If using a pot: cover and cook for 20–25 mins, stirring occasionally until soft and mushy.
6. Rest & Serve
    - Let it rest for 5 minutes after cooking. Adjust consistency with hot water if needed.
    - Drizzle a little ghee on top before serving.

Pari's Super Tips:

- Add a spoon of homemade curd on the side to boost probiotic content.
- For extra gut love, you can top with roasted pumpkin seeds or a squeeze of lemon.

Ideal as a light dinner or post-illness recovery meal.

Recipe 24 – Cooling Barnyard Millet Buttermilk

A Refreshing, Gut-Healing Drink

Barnyard Millet Buttermilk is a refreshing, probiotic-rich, and naturally cooling drink that is perfect for hot summers, digestion, and blood sugar control. This drink combines the goodness of barnyard millet (low GI, high fibre) with buttermilk (probiotics & hydration) to create a light yet nourishing beverage.

Ingredients (Serves 2-3)

- ¼ cup barnyard millet (soaked & cooked)
- 1 cup buttermilk (or whisked curd + ½ cup water)
- ½ tsp cumin powder (jeera, aids digestion)
- A pinch of rock salt (electrolyte balance)
- A few curry leaves (optional, enhances flavour & gut health)
- ½ tsp grated ginger (for digestion & metabolism boost)
- A handful of coriander leaves (for garnish, optional)
- 1 tsp lemon juice (for freshness, optional)

Step-by-Step Preparation

Step 1: Cook the Barnyard Millet

1. Rinse ¼ cup barnyard millet and soak it for 30 minutes.
2. In a pan, add ½ cup water and the soaked millet.
3. Cook on low-medium flame for 8-10 minutes, stirring occasionally, until soft.
4. Let it cool completely before using it in the buttermilk.

Step 2: Blend the Buttermilk Base

5. In a blender, add buttermilk (or whisked curd + water), cumin powder, salt, ginger, and curry leaves.
6. Blend for 10-15 seconds until frothy.

Step 3: Mix in the Cooked Barnyard Millet

7. Add the cooled barnyard millet to the blended buttermilk and stir well.
8. Squeeze in lemon juice (optional) for an extra refreshing taste.

Step 4: Serve & Enjoy!

9. Pour into glasses, garnish with coriander leaves, and serve chilled or at room temperature.

3 Different Variations of Barnyard Millet Buttermilk

1. **Spiced South Indian Version – Masala Neer Mor**
   ✓ Add:
   - A pinch of black salt & asafoetida (hing)
   - A few crushed green chilies & curry leaves
   - ½ tsp crushed mustard seeds for extra digestion benefits

   ✓ Why? A flavourful, spicy twist that aids digestion & metabolism.
2. **Mint & Cucumber Detox Buttermilk**
   ✓ Add:
   - 1 tbsp grated cucumber (hydration & cooling effect)
   - A handful of fresh mint leaves (detoxifying)
   - ½ tsp fennel seeds (saunf, for digestion & bloating relief)

   ✓ Why? A super-hydrating & cooling version ideal for hot summers.
3. **Protein-Packed Buttermilk with Sattu & Nuts**
   ✓ Add:
   - 1 tbsp sattu (roasted gram flour, for plant-based protein)
   - 1 tbsp crushed almonds or walnuts (healthy fats & protein)
   - ½ tsp honey (optional, natural sweetness & gut health)

   ✓ Why? This version keeps you full longer & is great post-workout or for energy boost.

Why You Should Try Barnyard Millet Buttermilk?

✓ Gut-Friendly & Probiotic-Rich – Supports digestion & gut microbiome.

✓ Cooling & Hydrating – Perfect for summer, prevents dehydration.

Conclusion:

The Science Behind Gut Health & Its Impact on Physical & Mental Well-being

1. Eat More Prebiotics & Probiotics – Feed the Good Bacteria
   - A study in *Nature Reviews Gastroenterology & Hepatology* (2020) found that consuming fermented foods and high-fibre prebiotic-rich diets increases gut bacterial diversity, improving digestion, metabolism, and immunity.
   - How to Apply? Include fermented foods (curd, kanji, kimchi, buttermilk, dosa, idli) and prebiotics (onions, garlic, bananas, millets, flaxseeds) in your diet.
2. Reduce Sugar & Processed Foods – Prevent Inflammation
   - Research in *The American Journal of Clinical Nutrition* (2021) found that high sugar and processed food intake reduces beneficial gut bacteria and increases inflammation, leading to metabolic disorders and mood imbalances.
   - How to Apply? Avoid refined sugars, sodas, junk food, and choose whole foods, natural sweeteners (dates, jaggery), and balanced meals.
3. Diversify Your Diet – A Wide Range of Foods Nourishes the Gut
   - The *Human Microbiome Project* (Harvard, 2020) showed that people who consume 30+ plant-based foods per week have better gut microbiome diversity than those with a limited diet.
   - How to Apply? Rotate millets, pulses, vegetables, seeds, nuts, and probiotic-rich foods for a healthier gut.
4. Stay Hydrated – Water is Essential for Gut Function
   - A study in *The Journal of Nutrition* (2019) found that dehydration disrupts gut flora, slows digestion, and increases gut permeability (leaky gut).
   - How to Apply? Drink 2-3 litres of water daily, including herbal teas, infused water, and coconut water.

5. Get Enough Sleep – Gut Health & Sleep are Linked
    - Research in *Cell Reports* (2021) shows that poor sleep disrupts gut bacteria balance, leading to hormonal imbalances, stress, and digestive issues.
    - How to Apply? Aim for 7-8 hours of restful sleep, avoid late-night eating, and establish a relaxing bedtime routine.

The Gut-Brain Connection – How Your Gut Affects Mental Health

Did you know that 90% of serotonin (the happiness hormone) is produced in the gut?

Your gut and brain are directly connected through the gut-brain axis, meaning that poor gut health can lead to mood disorders like anxiety, depression, and brain fog.

Scientific Evidence Linking Gut Health & Mental Health

1. Gut Microbiota Affects Mood & Stress Levels
    - A study published in *Nature Microbiology* (2022) found that people with diverse gut bacteria had lower stress levels and better mental resilience.
2. Probiotics Can Reduce Anxiety & Depression
    - Research in *The Journal of Psychiatric Research* (2020) showed that consuming probiotic-rich foods improved symptoms of depression and increased serotonin production.
3. Chronic Inflammation in the Gut Can Lead to Brain Fog & Fatigue
    - Studies in *Frontiers in Neuroscience* (2021) revealed that imbalanced gut bacteria can cause chronic inflammation, leading to cognitive issues and fatigue.

How to Improve Gut Health for Better Mental Well-being

- ☑ Eat More Probiotic-Rich Foods – Buttermilk, curd, kanji, fermented vegetables, and kombucha.
- ☑ Reduce Processed & Sugary Foods – These trigger gut inflammation and disrupt mental clarity.
- ☑ Manage Stress with Yoga & Meditation – Chronic stress alters gut microbiome balance.
- ☑ Get Daily Physical Activity – Exercise enhances gut bacteria diversity and reduces anxiety.
- ☑ Prioritize Good Sleep – Sleep restores gut function and balances hormones.

Final Takeaway: Gut Health = Whole-Body Health

Your gut is your second brain—take care of it, and it will take care of you.

SUCCESS STORY – 6

Radha's Story: From Constant Bloating to a Confident, Energised Life

---

When Radha first walked into AlaMirap Nutrition, she was exhausted. Not just physically, but mentally and emotionally too. She sighed as she sat down, pressing a hand to her abdomen, which had become a constant source of frustration.

"I wake up feeling bloated. I go to bed feeling bloated. I have tried everything—home remedies, skipping meals, even starving myself—but nothing works. I feel sluggish all day, and my stomach never feels light. What is wrong with me?"

Radha was tired of wearing loose clothes to hide her distended stomach. She was tired of declining social invitations because she felt uncomfortable. She was tired of feeling like her body was betraying her. She had always assumed that bloating was something she had to live with. But deep down, she hoped for a change.

The Turning Point: A New Approach to Food

We had seen hundreds of clients like Radha and could empathize. We sat with her, listened to her frustrations, and explained something that no one had told her before—her gut was inflamed, and her body was constantly fighting against her food choices. She wasn't eating "wrong" food; she was eating food that wasn't right for her body.

We first went ahead and got a gut microbiome test for her. While waiting for the results which would be handed within a week to 10 days, we encouraged her to take baby steps in setting her daily routine right.

After the test results of her gut microbiome test, she could see which foods she could use regularly, which she had to have in moderation, and the foods that she had to avoid. She was shocked to know that she could not have horse gram, peanuts, prawns as she had never felt uncomfortable with these foods before.

Based on her blood reports, we introduced her to an anti-inflammatory diet, a way of eating that was designed to heal her gut, reduce bloating, and restore her energy levels.

We introduced her to a Gut Restoration Diet for 4 weeks. There were food restrictions like no added sugars, fried foods, etc.

"Does that mean I can never eat my favourite foods again?"

We reassured her. This wasn't about restriction—it was about giving her body a break and letting it heal. She was really curious to know how her body would respond.

Month 1: Small Changes, Big Relief

The first thing Radha noticed was that she woke up feeling lighter. The morning bloating, which had been her daily reality for years, was suddenly gone. She called us, excited and hesitant at the same time. "Is it possible that this is working already?"

We encouraged her to stay consistent.

What Changed in Radha's Diet?

✓ She swapped wheat for millets—jowar, foxtail millet, and bajra, which are naturally gluten-free and easy on the gut.

✓ She cut out processed dairy and refined sugars, which had been triggering inflammation in her system.

✓ She added probiotic-rich foods—homemade curd, fermented vegetables, and kanji—to restore her gut microbiome.

✓ She started her mornings with turmeric water and cumin tea, instead of tea with sugar and milk.

One week turned into two.

Her energy levels improved. She no longer felt like she needed a nap after every meal. Her bloating reduced drastically, and she started noticing a slight change in her waistline. She didn't feel sluggish anymore. For the first time in years, she felt in control of her body, rather than trapped in it.

Month 2: The Glow of Confidence – Gut Maintenance Diet

By the second month, Radha had become obsessed with how good she felt.

Her skin looked clearer, her digestion was smooth, and she felt stronger, lighter, and more confident. She had always thought that her body was working against her, but now she realised that her body had been crying for help all along. She stepped onto the weighing scale—not expecting much, because weight loss was not her goal.

To her surprise, she had lost inches from her abdomen. She sent a message: "For the first time in years, I feel comfortable wearing my favourite dress again."

But the most beautiful change?

She started smiling more. She stopped obsessing over her food and started enjoying the process of nourishing her body. She went from saying, "I can't eat that," to "I don't even feel like eating that anymore."

Month 3: A Transformation Beyond the Mirror

By the third month, Radha had completely embraced this new way of eating.

She no longer needed to rely on food to comfort her. She no longer feared bloating after every meal. She looked at herself in the mirror and felt something she hadn't felt in a long time—pride. Her family noticed it too.

Her husband told her, "You look so much happier these days." Her friends asked, "What have you been doing? You look amazing!" But the biggest win was what she told herself: "I am finally taking care of myself."

For years, she had lived with gut issues, thinking it was normal. But now she knew better. She had rewritten her story, and this time, her body was on her side.

What Radha Learned About the Anti-Inflammatory Diet

1. Food is Medicine – Healing starts from within. The right foods can reduce inflammation, improve digestion, and restore energy.
2. Bloating is NOT Normal – It is a sign that the gut needs support. Simple swaps, like switching to millets and fermented foods, can transform digestion.
3. Weight Loss is a Side Effect of Good Health – When you nourish your body, it rewards you. Radha did not diet to lose weight—she healed her gut, and the weight loss happened naturally.

Radha's Takeaway

"I came to AlaMirap thinking I had to live with gut issues forever. I left with more than just a better diet—I left with a new relationship with my body. I feel like myself again."

Are You Struggling with Gut Issues Like Radha?

- Do you experience constant bloating and indigestion?
- Do you feel sluggish, tired, or out of sync with your body?
- Have you tried everything but nothing seems to work?

Time For Change – Your Body is not broken – It just needs to heal.

7 -Vinay's Journey: From Overweight and Exhausted to Fit and Fearless

Vinay had always been the fun, easy-going guy in his college group, but beneath his cheerful personality, he carried a burden no one saw—his weight. At 5 feet 8 inches and 120 kilos, he struggled with constant fatigue, low energy, and self-doubt.

Late-night junk food, frequent takeaways, and zero time for exercise had become his normal. He laughed along with his friends when they joked about his size, but deep inside, he wished he could change. One evening, at a family gathering, his five-year-old niece looked at him with innocent eyes and said,

"Vinay chachu, if you eat more, you might burst like a balloon!"

Everyone laughed. But something inside Vinay shifted. He forced a smile, but in that moment, he knew—enough was enough. He didn't want to be the "funny fat guy" anymore. He wanted to be strong, confident, and most importantly, healthy.

That day, he made a decision. It wouldn't be a quick fix. It wouldn't be easy.

But he was ready to fight for himself.

With this determination he reached out to us.

Month 1: Facing Reality & Taking the First Step

- Vinay's first challenge wasn't the workouts or diet—it was changing his mindset.
- The first time he stepped on the treadmill, he could barely run for a minute.
- The first time he tried cutting out junk food, the cravings were unbearable.
- The first time he saw his reflection in the gym mirror, he wanted to quit.

But he didn't.

Instead, we helped him focus on small wins. Consistency and his efforts to change.

✓ Portion Control – He didn't stop eating his favourite foods but learned to eat mindfully.

✓ Cutting Out Sugary Drinks – No more colas, artificial juices, or extra sugar in tea/coffee.

✓ Walking 5,000 Steps Daily – He started with just 15 minutes, gradually increasing.

✓ Drinking More Water – He realised most of his cravings were actually dehydration.

At the end of four weeks, he had lost 4 kilos. It wasn't much, but for the first time, he felt in control.

Month 4: The First Big Wins

Vinay had reduced by 12 kilos at the end of 4 months. His clothes size reduced. He could shop in regular shops from PLUS size stores. His face looked sharper, and he had more energy than ever. His friends noticed. His family noticed. Most importantly, he noticed. The guy who used to wake up feeling sluggish now woke up ready to take on the day. What Kept Him Going?

✓ Switching to Millets & High-Fibre Foods – Instead of rice, he ate jowar rotis, bajra khichdi, and foxtail millet dosa.

✓ Strength Training & Cardio – He started lifting weights 3 times a week and doing HIIT workouts.

✓ Sleeping on Time – Late-night binges were replaced by seven hours of proper sleep.

But the biggest change?

He stopped seeing this as a "diet" and started seeing it as a lifestyle.

Vinay's journey proved that change is possible. It doesn't happen overnight. It doesn't come easy. But if you decide to take charge, there is no limit to how much you can transform.

Vinay's Advice to Anyone Struggling with Weight Loss

1. Start Small – You don't have to change everything at once. Begin with one habit at a time.
2. Be Patient – It took years to gain weight, so don't expect to lose it in a month.

3. Find What Works for You – Not all diets and workouts are the same. Make it sustainable.
4. Stay Consistent – Motivation fades, but discipline keeps you going.
5. Do It for Yourself – Not for looks, not for validation—for your health and happiness.

Vinay continued on his fat loss journey and his most special day was when his scales from 3 digits – 120 kilos - came down to 99 by the end of 9 months.

It reiterated that – anything is possible – once you DECIDE

Are You Ready to Transform Like Vinay? If you are struggling with weight, feeling stuck, or wondering if change is possible—let this story be your proof.

The first step is the hardest. But once you take it, you won't want to stop.

Chapter 6

WOMEN'S WELLNESS

"Taking care of yourself doesn't mean me first. It means me too."
– L.R. Knost

Women's health is often a balancing act—juggling multiple roles while caring for loved ones, managing work, and trying to find time for self-care. In the rush of daily life, self-care can easily take a back seat, leading to fatigue, stress, and various health issues. Whether dealing with hormonal changes, managing menstrual health, navigating pregnancy, or embracing menopause, the body requires specific nutrients to function optimally.

Nutrient Powerhouses for Women's Health

Iron and Folate for Energy and Vitality

Women are more prone to anaemia due to menstruation, pregnancy, and menopause. Millets such as finger millet (ragi) and pearl millet (bajra) are rich in iron and folate, helping to maintain healthy haemoglobin levels and combat fatigue. They support energy levels, improve mental clarity, and enhance overall vitality.

Calcium and Magnesium for Bone Health

Bone health is crucial, especially during pregnancy and menopause when calcium requirements increase. Ragi is particularly high in calcium, and millets like foxtail millet provide magnesium, which enhances calcium absorption and supports muscle function.

Fibre and Antioxidants for Hormonal Balance

The high fibre content in millets aids digestion and helps balance hormones by regulating insulin levels. Sorghum (jowar) and little millet are excellent for maintaining hormonal health, reducing premenstrual symptoms, and easing menopausal discomfort.

B-Vitamins for Stress Relief and Mood Support

Stress and mood swings are common due to hormonal fluctuations. Millets are rich in B-vitamins, especially niacin (B3) and pyridoxine (B6), which play a key role in serotonin production, helping to improve mood and reduce stress.

Millets provide complete nourishment that supports a woman's body at every stage of life. Incorporating them into the diet is not just about eating—it is an investment in long-term health and well-being.

Scientific Evidence on Women's Hormonal Health

Hormonal imbalances are closely linked to diet, as processed foods, sugar, and nutrient deficiencies can disrupt hormone regulation. Millets, rich in fibre, essential minerals, and complex carbohydrates, help balance blood sugar, improve gut health, and support overall hormonal stability naturally.

Studies indicate that one in five young Indian women suffer from Polycystic Ovary Syndrome (PCOS), which is higher than the global average. Additionally, menstrual disorders such as dysmenorrhea (painful menstruation) affect a significant portion of Indian women, with prevalence rates ranging from 46 to 66 percent. These variations highlight the need for increased awareness and dietary intervention to support hormonal health effectively.

Five Evidence-Based Methods to Improve Women's Health

1. Prioritise Quality Sleep
   - Maintain a consistent sleep schedule (seven to nine hours).
   - Avoid screens and caffeine at least one hour before bed.
   - Create a relaxing bedtime routine, such as reading or meditation.
   - Sleep helps regulate hormones, reduces stress, and supports mental clarity.
2. Stay Active and Move Daily
   - Aim for 30 minutes of movement, including walking, yoga, or strength training.
   - Find an activity that is enjoyable to stay consistent.
   - Exercise improves mood, supports weight management, and reduces premenstrual symptoms.
3. Manage Stress Mindfully
   - Practice deep breathing, meditation, or journaling.
   - Engage in hobbies and self-care.

- Set healthy boundaries to protect mental peace.
- Reducing stress prevents hormonal imbalances, mood swings, and emotional fatigue.

4. Eat Mindfully and Stay Hydrated
   - Focus on whole foods—millets, legumes, vegetables, and healthy fats.
   - Eat slowly and listen to hunger cues to prevent overeating.
   - Drink two to three litres of water daily for hydration.
   - Proper nutrition prevents hormonal fluctuations, stabilises blood sugar, and improves skin and metabolism.
5. Prioritise Hormonal Balance
   - Include millets, seeds (flax, chia), and iron-rich foods.
   - Reduce processed foods and excessive sugar.
   - Monitor menstrual health and seek expert guidance if needed.
   - Balanced hormones support energy levels, emotional stability, and overall health.

Final Thought

A balanced lifestyle is not about perfection—it is about small, sustainable changes that lead to lasting wellness.

Health is like fuel for the body. Just as a car struggles to function on low fuel, the body slows down without proper nutrition, rest, and self-care.

Prioritising health is not selfish—it is necessary.

Every time you choose to nourish your body with whole foods and mindful habits, you are choosing better health, balance, and well-being.

Invest in yourself today—your future self will thank you.

Sharing two powerful millet-based smoothies that help balance hormones naturally. These smoothies incorporate hormone-friendly ingredients like flaxseeds, nuts, and plant-based proteins while keeping them delicious and easy to make.

Recipe 25 – Hormone-Balancing Ragi (Finger Millet) Almond Smoothie

This smoothie helps regulate estrogen levels, support thyroid function, and reduce stress-related hormonal imbalances.

Ingredients:

- 2 tbsp ragi (finger millet) flour
- 1 cup almond milk (or any plant-based milk)
- 1 banana (for natural sweetness and potassium)
- 1 tbsp flaxseeds (rich in lignans that balance estrogen)
- 5 soaked almonds (for healthy fats and vitamin E)
- 1 tbsp peanut butter (for protein and healthy fats)
- ½ tsp cinnamon powder (helps regulate insulin levels)
- ½ tsp cocoa powder (optional, for a chocolatey flavour)
- 1 tsp honey (optional, for added sweetness)
- Ice cubes (as needed)

Directions:

1. Prepare the ragi base: In a pan, dry roast the ragi flour for 2 minutes on low heat. Add ¼ cup warm water, mix well to make a paste, and let it cool.
2. Blend the ingredients: In a blender, add almond milk, banana, flaxseeds, soaked almonds, peanut butter, cinnamon, cocoa powder, and honey.
3. Add the ragi paste: Blend again until smooth.
4. Serve: Pour into a glass, add ice cubes, and enjoy!

Benefits:

- Ragi is rich in calcium, iron, and amino acids that help regulate hormone production. Flaxseeds provide omega-3 fatty acids, which support hormonal balance. Almonds and peanut butter help regulate cortisol (stress hormone) and provide sustained energy.

Recipe 26 – Little Millet Hormone Harmony Smoothie

What It Does

This smoothie is designed to help balance hormones, support insulin sensitivity, and provide gentle fiber—all crucial for managing PCOS. The inclusion of little millet adds slow-digesting carbohydrates and additional fiber, keeping you fuller longer and aiding in blood sugar control.

Ingredients (1 Serving)

- **Fresh Fruits & Flavors:**
  - **Papaya:** ½ cup, diced

    Benefits: Rich in enzymes and antioxidants, aiding digestion and detoxification.
  - **Banana:** 1 small (preferably the local variety)

    Benefits: Provides natural sweetness, potassium, and energy.
  - **Pomegranate Seeds:** 2 tablespoons

    Benefits: Packed with antioxidants and phytonutrients that support hormonal balance.
- **Millet & Seeds:**
  - **Cooked & Cooled Little Millet (Saamai):** 2 tablespoons

    Benefits: Low glycaemic index, excellent fiber, and nutrients to help manage insulin resistance.
  - **Flaxseeds:** 1 tablespoon (soaked for at least 2 hours or overnight)

    Benefits: Rich in omega-3 fatty acids and lignans which support estrogen balance.

- **Nuts & Liquids:**
    - **Almonds:** 5, soaked and peeled

      Benefits: Provide healthy fats and a dose of protein for satiety.
    - **Fresh Coconut Water:** ½ cup

      Benefits: Hydration with natural electrolytes and a subtle tropical flavor.
- **Spices & Optional Adaptogens:**
    - **Cinnamon Powder:** ¼ teaspoon

      Benefits: Helps regulate blood sugar levels and improve insulin sensitivity.
    - **Ashwagandha Powder (Optional):** ½ teaspoon

      Benefits: An adaptogen that supports stress reduction and hormonal balance.
- **Extras:**
    - **Ice Cubes:** A few, if you prefer a chilled smoothie

Step-by-Step Preparation

1. **Prep the Millet:**
    - **Cook Little Millet:** Rinse ¼ cup of little millet thoroughly. Combine with about ⅝ cup water (using a 1:2.5 ratio) in a small saucepan. Bring to a boil, then reduce the heat, cover, and simmer until the millet is soft (about 15–20 minutes). Allow it to cool completely before adding to the smoothie.
2. **Prepare the Flaxseeds & Almonds:**
    - **Soak Flaxseeds:** Soak 1 tablespoon of flaxseeds in water for at least 2 hours (or overnight) to soften them, which aids digestion and nutrient absorption.
    - **Soak Almonds:** Soak 5 almonds for 4–6 hours or overnight, then peel to remove the skin for a smoother texture.

3. **Combine Ingredients:**
    - Add the diced papaya, banana, and pomegranate seeds into your blender.
    - Include the cooled little millet, soaked flaxseeds (with any water drained), and peeled almonds.
    - Sprinkle in the cinnamon powder and, if using, the ashwagandha powder.
    - Pour in the fresh coconut water.
    - Add a few ice cubes if you desire a colder drink.
4. **Blend:** Blend on high speed until you achieve a smooth, creamy consistency. If the smoothie is too thick, you can add a splash more coconut water until it reaches your desired texture.
5. **Serve & Enjoy:** Pour the smoothie into a glass and enjoy immediately on an empty stomach in the morning for the best absorption of nutrients.

Additional Tips

- **Consistency Tip:** If you prefer a thicker smoothie, you can reduce the amount of coconut water or add more cooled millet. For a thinner consistency, simply add more liquid.
- **Nutrient Boost:** You can blend in a handful of spinach for extra greens without altering the taste significantly.
- **Storage:** For the best flavor and nutrient retention, drink the smoothie right after preparation.

Enjoy this nutrient-packed, hormone-balancing smoothie as part of your morning routine to help manage PCOS and support overall hormonal health!

Let's Try Amazing Millet Breakfasts

Recipe 27 – Breakfast: Sprouted Ragi (Finger Millet) & Nut Porridge

A warm and **comforting porridge** packed with **iron, calcium, and omega-3 fatty acids** to support **hormonal health**.

Ingredients:

- ½ cup **sprouted ragi flour**
- 1 cup **almond milk or coconut milk**
- 1 tbsp **flaxseeds (ground)**
- 1 tbsp **pumpkin seeds** (rich in zinc for hormone regulation)
- 1 tbsp **chopped walnuts** (for omega-3 and brain health)
- 1 **small banana** (for potassium and energy)
- 1 tsp **jaggery powder or honey**
- ½ tsp **cinnamon powder** (balances blood sugar)

Directions:

- **Roast ragi flour** in a pan for 2 minutes on low heat.
- **Add almond milk** and cook for 5 minutes until thickened.
- **Add flaxseeds, pumpkin seeds, walnuts, and mashed banana**. Stir well.
- **Sweeten with jaggery/honey** and add cinnamon for flavour.
- **Serve warm** for sustained energy and stable hormones.

Benefits:

- **Ragi** is rich in **calcium, iron, and amino acids** that support **estrogen balance**.
- **Flaxseeds and walnuts** provide **omega-3 fatty acids**, helping **reduce PMS symptoms and inflammation**.
- **Pumpkin seeds** help **boost progesterone levels**.

Recipe 28 – Foxtail Millet Bisi Bele Bath (Hormone-Balancing Recipe)

This **South Indian-style Bisi Bele Bath** replaces rice with **foxtail millet**, making it a **fiber-rich, blood sugar-friendly, and hormone-supportive meal**. It's packed with **protein, healthy fats, and gut-friendly spices**, making it perfect for those dealing with **PCOS, thyroid imbalances, or insulin resistance**.

Ingredients:

For the Millet & Dal Base:

- ½ cup **foxtail millet** (soaked for 4 to 6 hours)
- ¼ cup **toor dal (pigeon pea lentils)**
- ½ tsp **turmeric powder**
- 2 cups **water**
- Salt to taste

For the Bisi Bele Bath Masala (Spice Blend) – ingredients listed below

For the Vegetable Mix:

- 1 cup **mixed vegetables** (carrots, beans, peas, drumsticks, brinjal, capsicum)
- 1 tbsp **ghee** or **cold-pressed coconut oil**
- 1 tsp **mustard seeds**
- 1 sprig **curry leaves**
- 1 small **tamarind ball** (soaked in warm water, extract the pulp)

For Garnish:

- 1 tbsp **roasted peanuts** or **cashews**
- 1 tbsp **coriander leaves**
- ½ tsp **ghee** (optional)

Step-by-Step Directions

Step 1: Cook the Millet & Dal

1. **Rinse foxtail millet and toor dal** separately.
2. **Cook them together** in a pressure cooker with 2 cups water, turmeric, and salt. Cook for **3-4 whistles** or until soft. Mash lightly and set aside.

Step 2: Prepare the Masala Powder

1. **Dry roast** coriander seeds, chana dal, urad dal, red chilies, fenugreek, cumin, mustard seeds, black peppercorns, cloves, cinnamon, sesame seeds, and grated coconut in a pan until aromatic. **Cool and grind into a fine powder.**

Step 3: Cook the Vegetables

1. Heat **ghee or coconut oil** in a deep pan.
2. Add **mustard seeds** and let them splutter.
3. Add **curry leaves** and sauté for 10 seconds.
4. Add **chopped vegetables** and sauté for 3-4 minutes.
5. Add **tamarind extract** and cook for 5 minutes.

Step 4: Combine Everything

1. Add the **cooked millet-dal mixture** to the vegetable pan.
2. Stir in the **prepared masala powder** and mix well.
3. Simmer for **5-7 minutes**, adding water if needed to adjust consistency.

Step 5: Garnish & Serve

Top with **roasted peanuts or cashews** for crunch. Add **a spoon of ghee** for extra flavour and digestion support. Garnish with **fresh coriander leaves** and serve warm.

Why This Recipe is Great for Hormonal Balance

- ☑ **Foxtail Millet**: High in fiber, stabilises blood sugar, and supports thyroid function.
- ☑ **Fenugreek & Sesame Seeds**: Help balance estrogen levels and improve insulin sensitivity.
- ☑ **Curry Leaves & Tamarind**: Aid liver detox, helping with hormone metabolism.
- ☑ **Toor Dal & Peanuts**: Provide plant-based protein and support **progesterone production**.

Recipe 29 – Chinese-Style Barnyard Millet Stir-Fried Vegetables

This **Chinese-style stir-fried barnyard millet** is a **healthy, flavourful, and hormone-friendly alternative to fried rice**. It's packed with **fiber, antioxidants, and plant-based proteins**, making it perfect for **balancing hormones, reducing inflammation, and improving digestion**.

Ingredients:

For Cooking the Millet

- 1 cup **barnyard millet (soaked for 2 to 4 hours, drained)**
- 2 cups **water**
- ½ tsp **salt**

For the Stir-Fry

- 1 tbsp **sesame oil** (rich in zinc & healthy fats for hormone health)
- 1 tsp **ginger, finely chopped**
- 1 tsp **garlic, finely chopped**
- ½ cup **onion, finely sliced**
- ½ cup **carrots, julienned**
- ½ cup **capsicum (red, green, yellow), thinly sliced**
- ½ cup **broccoli florets**
- ½ cup **cabbage, shredded**
- 2 tbsp **spring onions, chopped**
- 1 tbsp **soya sauce (use tamari for gluten-free option)**
- 1 tsp **rice vinegar** (helps digestion)
- 1 tsp **black pepper powder**
- ½ tsp **red chilli flakes** (optional, for spice)
- 1 tbsp **toasted sesame seeds** (hormone-balancing properties)
- 1 tbsp **cashews or almonds (optional, for crunch)**

Step-by-Step Directions

Step 1: Cook the Millet

1. Boil **2 cups water** with a pinch of salt.
2. Add **barnyard millet** and simmer until soft and fluffy (about 10 minutes).
3. Fluff with a fork and let it cool completely (for the best stir-fry texture).

Step 2: Stir-Fry the Vegetables

1. Heat **sesame oil** in a large pan or wok on high heat.
2. Add **chopped ginger and garlic**, sauté until fragrant.
3. Add **onions** and stir-fry for 1 minute.
4. Add **carrots, capsicum, broccoli, and cabbage**, stir-fry for 3-4 minutes on high heat (vegetables should stay crunchy).

Step 3: Add Millet & Sauces

1. Add the **cooked barnyard millet** to the wok.
2. Pour in **soya sauce, rice vinegar, black pepper, and red chilli flakes**.
3. Stir-fry on high heat for 2 minutes, tossing everything well.

Step 4: Garnish & Serve

Sprinkle with **toasted sesame seeds, spring onions, and cashews/ almonds** for extra crunch. Serve hot with a side of **chilli sauce or a bowl of warm soup**.

Why This Recipe is Great for Hormonal Balance

☑ **Barnyard Millet**: High in **fiber and B-vitamins**, stabilising **blood sugar** and supporting **thyroid health**.

☑ **Sesame Seeds & Sesame Oil**: Provide **zinc and lignans**, essential for **balancing estrogen levels**.

☑ **Broccoli & Cabbage**: Cruciferous vegetables help **detox excess estrogen** from the body.

☑ **Soya Sauce (or Tamari)**: Contains **natural phytoestrogens**, supporting **hormonal health**.

☑ **Garlic & Ginger**: Reduce **inflammation** and support **liver detoxification**.

Recipe 30 – Crispy Millet Bhel Puri – A Guilt-Free, Hormone-Balancing Chaat

This millet-based Bhel Puri is a crunchy, tangy, and nutrient-packed snack that satisfies your chaat cravings while supporting hormonal balance. We replace puffed rice with roasted millets to make it fiber-rich, blood sugar-friendly, and full of gut-healthy ingredients.

Ingredients:

For the Millet Base

- ½ cup foxtail millet or barnyard millet (dry roasted)
- ¼ cup puffed jowar (sorghum) or puffed bajra (pearl millet)
- ¼ cup roasted chana dal (split chickpeas)

For the Chaat Mix

- ½ cup cucumber, finely chopped
- ½ cup tomatoes, finely chopped (remove seeds to prevent sogginess)
- ½ cup onion, finely chopped
- ½ cup boiled moong sprouts (for protein and gut health)
- ¼ cup grated carrot (adds fiber & beta-carotene)
- ¼ cup pomegranate seeds (natural sweetness & antioxidants)
- 1 green chili, finely chopped (optional, for spice)
- 1 tbsp coriander leaves, chopped
- 1 tbsp roasted peanuts or almonds (for crunch & healthy fats)

For the Tangy Dressing

- 1 tbsp tamarind chutney (sweet & tangy flavour)
- 1 tsp green chutney (mint-coriander chutney)
- ½ tsp black salt (kala namak)
- ½ tsp chaat masala
- ½ tsp roasted cumin powder
- Juice of ½ lemon (for freshness & digestion)

For Garnish

- 1 tbsp toasted sesame seeds (zinc & hormone support)
- ½ cup baked millet crisps or roasted makhana (fox nuts) for extra crunch
- 1 tbsp sev (optional, for authentic chaat texture)

Step-by-Step Directions

Step 1: Prepare the Millet Base

1. Dry roast foxtail or barnyard millet in a pan for 2-3 minutes until slightly crispy. Let it cool.
2. Mix with puffed jowar or bajra and roasted chana dal. Set aside.

Step 2: Assemble the Chaat Mix

1. In a large bowl, combine cucumber, tomatoes, onions, carrots, moong sprouts, and pomegranate seeds.
2. Toss in green chili, coriander leaves, and roasted peanuts/almonds.

Step 3: Add the Dressing

1. In a small bowl, mix tamarind chutney, green chutney, black salt, chaat masala, cumin powder, and lemon juice. Pour the dressing over the chaat mix and toss well.
2. Just before serving, mix in the crispy millet base to keep the chaat crunchy.
3. Garnish with toasted sesame seeds, millet crisps, and a sprinkle of sev.
4. Serve immediately with an extra squeeze of lemon.

Why This Recipe is Great for Hormonal Balance

☑ Millets (Foxtail/Barnyard): High in fiber and slow-releasing carbs, stabilising blood sugar and insulin levels.

☑ Sesame Seeds & Peanuts: Rich in zinc and magnesium, essential for balancing estrogen and progesterone.

☑ Moong Sprouts: Provide plant-based protein, essential for thyroid health.

☑ Pomegranate & Lemon: Support liver detox, helping with hormonal metabolism.

☑ Cumin & Black Salt: Aid digestion and reduce bloating.

SUCCESS STORY - 7

Ananya's Journey to Hormonal Balance

Ananya, a **29-year-old working professional**, walked into **Alamirap Nutrition** looking exhausted. **"I feel like a mess,"** she admitted. **"My periods are irregular, PMS is unbearable, and I'm tired all the time. I've tried everything—painkillers, sugar cravings, even skipping workouts—but nothing works long-term."**

I could see the frustration in her eyes. Like many women, she was caught in a cycle of **temporary relief, followed by recurring problems**. **Hormonal imbalances** had taken over her life, and she was desperate for a real solution.

The Turning Point: Introducing Millets & Lifestyle Tweaks

At **Alamirap Nutrition**, we guided Ananya through a **personalised plan** focused on:

✓ **Balancing her meals with millets** – Ragi, foxtail, and bajra to stabilise blood sugar & hormones.

✓ **Boosting iron & protein intake** – To combat fatigue and support overall health.

✓ **Cutting down refined sugar & processed foods** – To prevent PMS flare-ups.

✓ **Adding mindful movement & relaxation** – Yoga, deep breathing, and better sleep habits.

At first, she hesitated. **"Millets? Won't they be dry and boring?"** she asked.

We laughed and shared multiple links to millet recipes.

"Try it for a week. If you don't feel the difference, we'll talk."

Month 1: Small Changes, Big Impact

Ananya followed the plan with **mild scepticism**, but within weeks, she noticed:

☑ **More energy, fewer cravings** – She didn't feel the need for her usual sugary tea breaks.

☑ **Less bloating & PMS relief** – No more extreme mood swings or unbearable cramps.

☑ **Stable digestion** – No more gut discomfort from processed foods.

By the **second month**, she was hooked! **She had her first regular cycle in years.**

Month 3: A Total Transformation

By the third month, Ananya walked into our office **glowing with confidence. "I can't believe this is me! I feel normal again."**

Her wins:

✓ **No more irregular periods** – Her cycle was on track.

✓ **No need for painkillers** – PMS symptoms had reduced drastically.

✓ **Sustainable weight loss** – Without extreme diets or restrictions.

✓ **Better mood & focus** – No more energy crashes.

Ananya's Verdict

"I came in looking for a solution and found a **lifestyle change that truly works**. AlaMirap didn't just give me a diet—they helped me regain control over my body and health. Millets weren't just food for me; they became my **healing fuel**."

Through **small, mindful changes**, Ananya **transformed her health naturally**, proving that when you nourish your body the right way, it **rewards you in the best ways possible!**

Remember, **hormonal imbalances** are closely linked to **diet**, as **processed foods, sugar, and nutrient deficiencies** ✕ can disrupt **hormone**

regulation. Millets, rich in **fibre, essential minerals, and complex carbs**, ☑ help **balance blood sugar**, improve **gut health**, and support overall **hormonal stability** naturally.

Struggling with hormonal imbalances?

Hormonal disorders, such as **Polycystic Ovary Syndrome (PCOS)**, are prevalent among Indian women, with studies indicating varying rates:

- A meta-analysis found a pooled prevalence of approximately **11.33%** using Rotterdam's criteria. pmc.ncbi.nlm.nih.gov
- Some reports suggest that **1 in 5** young Indian women suffer from PCOS, which is higher than the global average of 8% to 13%. thinkglobalhealth.org

Additionally, menstrual disorders, such as **dysmenorrhea (painful menstruation)**, affect a significant portion of Indian women, with prevalence rates ranging from **46% to 66.7%**. en.wikipedia.org

These variations highlight the need for standardized diagnostic criteria and increased awareness to effectively address hormonal health issues among Indian women.

"Your hormones are talking to you. Listen, nourish, and thrive."

Hormonal Imbalances in Men:

Causes, Symptoms & Most Common Issues

Hormones play a crucial role in a man's body, regulating energy levels, muscle mass, mood, libido, metabolism, and overall well-being. However, certain imbalances can lead to serious health issues if not addressed.

Most Common Hormonal Imbalance in Men

Low Testosterone (Hypogonadism) – The most frequent hormonal issue in men, affecting energy levels, mood, muscle strength, libido, and metabolism.

Symptoms of Low Testosterone:

- Fatigue & Low Energy Levels
- Reduced Muscle Mass & Increased Fat (especially around the belly)
- Decreased Libido & Erectile Dysfunction
- Mood Swings, Irritability, or Depression
- Hair Thinning or Loss
- Difficulty Concentrating ("Brain Fog")
- Weaker Bones & Increased Risk of Osteoporosis

When Does It Occur?

- After 30: Testosterone naturally declines by 1% per year after age 30.
- Mid-40s to 50s: More noticeable symptoms of andropause (male menopause).
- Obese Men & Those with Chronic Stress: Faster decline due to insulin resistance, cortisol imbalances, and poor lifestyle habits.

Other Common Hormonal Imbalances in Men

1. **High Cortisol (Chronic Stress Hormone Imbalance)**
    - Occurs Most in Men Aged 25–50 (High-stress careers, lack of sleep, excessive caffeine).
    - Symptoms:
        - Constant Fatigue & Poor Sleep. Increased Belly Fat & Sugar Cravings.
        - High Blood Pressure & Anxiety. Weakened Immune System
    - Causes:
        - Chronic stress (work, financial, relationship pressures).
        - Overuse of caffeine, alcohol, or processed foods.
        - Excessive cardio or overtraining (raises cortisol & lowers testosterone).
2. **Estrogen Dominance (High Estrogen in Men)**
    - Occurs in Men Aged 35–60 (Often linked to obesity, poor liver detox, and processed food intake).

- Symptoms:
  - Increased Belly Fat & Chest Fat ("Man Boobs") Low Libido & Erectile Issues
  - Mood Swings & Anxiety. Hair Loss & Water Retention
- Causes:
  - Excess Body Fat (fat cells convert testosterone into estrogen).
  - Poor Liver Health (slows down estrogen detox).
  - Plastic & Processed Foods (BPA, soy-based processed foods).

3. **Insulin Resistance (Pre-Diabetes & Metabolic Issues)**
   - Most Common in Men Aged 30–50 (Linked to a high-carb diet & sedentary lifestyle).
   - Symptoms:
     - Constant Hunger & Sugar Cravings. Fat Gain (Especially Around the Waist)
     - Low Energy & Brain Fog. Skin Darkening (Acanthosis Nigricans on Neck/Armpits)
     - Difficulty Losing weight Despite Dieting
   - Causes:
     - High sugar & refined carb intake (fast food, sodas).
     - Lack of exercise & poor sleep.
     - Chronic stress increasing cortisol levels.

4. **Thyroid Imbalances (Hypothyroidism in Men)**
   - Most Common in Men Over 40 (Also seen in younger men with autoimmune conditions).
   - Symptoms:
     - Slower Metabolism & Weight Gain
     - Fatigue & Low Motivation
     - Hair Thinning & Dry Skin
     - Feeling Cold Often
     - Constipation & Digestive Issues
   - Causes:
     - Iodine or Selenium Deficiency (nutritional imbalances).
     - Chronic Stress & High Cortisol (inhibits thyroid function).
     - Autoimmune Issues (Hashimoto's Thyroiditis in some cases).

What Age Groups Are Most Affected?

☑ Men in Their 20s & 30s – Stress-driven high cortisol & low testosterone due to poor lifestyle habits.

☑ Men in Their 40s & 50s – Natural testosterone decline, insulin resistance, and estrogen dominance.

☑ Men Over 60 – Higher risk of hypothyroidism, severe testosterone drop, and osteoporosis.

How to Fix Hormonal Imbalances in Men Naturally

☑ Exercise Regularly – Strength training boosts testosterone & lowers cortisol/insulin resistance.

☑ Eat a Hormone-Friendly Diet –

☑ Fix Sleep – 7-8 hours to restore hormone levels.

☑ Reduce Stress – Meditation, deep breathing, cold showers.

☑ Limit Sugar & Alcohol – Reduces insulin spikes & prevents testosterone drops.

SUCCESS STORY – 8

Meet Raghav (Age 38) – A Stressed-Out Tech Professional

Background: Raghav, a 38-year-old software engineer from Bengaluru, approached **AlaMirap Nutrition** feeling **constantly fatigued, gaining belly fat, and experiencing low motivation**.

- **Symptoms:**
  - ☑ Low energy & brain fog
  - ☑ Weight gain, especially around the belly
  - ☑ Reduced muscle mass despite gym workouts
  - ☑ Cravings for sugar & caffeine to stay awake
  - ☑ Mood swings, irritability, and poor sleep

- **Diagnosis:**
  - 🔴 **High Cortisol & Low Testosterone** (caused by chronic stress & poor diet)
  - 🔴 **Insulin Resistance** (due to excessive carbs & lack of fiber)

The Alamirap Nutrition Strategy: Lifestyle & Diet Fixes

Step 1: Fixing His Diet (Millet-Based Hormone-Balancing Plan)

Instead of **refined carbs (white rice, bread, sugary snacks)**, we introduced complex carbohydrates like millets.

Step 2: Lifestyle Changes for Hormone Balance

1. **Sleep Optimization**
   - Set a strict **10:30 PM bedtime**
   - No **phone/laptop after 9 PM** (to prevent blue-light cortisol spikes)
   - 5 minutes of **meditation & deep breathing** before bed
2. **Stress Management**
   - **Morning walk (30 min in sunlight)** to boost **Vitamin D & testosterone**
   - Cold showers to lower **cortisol**
   - Daily **5-minute journaling** to reduce mental stress
3. **Exercise Plan (Boost Testosterone Naturally)**
   - ☑ **Strength training 3x per week** (focus on heavy compound lifts)
   - ☑ **Yoga & Stretching** on rest days (reduces cortisol & aids recovery)
   - ☑ **Avoiding excessive cardio** (keeps testosterone levels high)

Results After 3 Months with AlaMirap

✓ **Lost 5 kg of belly fat & gained lean muscle**

✓ **Energy levels improved, no more afternoon crashes**

✓ **Better sleep & mood stability**

✓ **Testosterone levels increased naturally**

✓ **Reduced sugar cravings & better digestion**

How AlaMirap Helped Raghav Take Control of His Health

☑ **Personalized Nutrition Plan:** Focused on **millets, protein, and hormone-friendly foods.**

☑ **Millet-Based Recipes:** Easy-to-make meals that **stabilized his insulin & improved gut health.**

☑ **Lifestyle Adjustments:** Simple, **sustainable changes** to **reduce stress & boost testosterone**.

☑ **Ongoing Support:** Weekly **check-ins with a dietitian** to keep him accountable.

Key Takeaway

- Hormonal imbalance is **not just about medication—it's about lifestyle, nutrition, and mindset.**
- **A millet-based diet + stress reduction + strength training = natural hormone balance.**
- **Alamirap Nutrition** helps men like Raghav **achieve lasting hormonal health** through **science-backed, traditional Indian food solutions.**

Men often ignore hormonal imbalances, mistaking them for aging or stress, but issues like low testosterone, high cortisol, and insulin resistance can severely impact health. If you're experiencing fatigue, weight gain, mood swings, or low libido, consult a doctor for hormone testing and seek expert nutrition guidance to restore balance naturally.

"Strong Men, Strong Families – Take Charge of Your Health Today!"

Chapter 7

LATEST TECHNOLOGIES TRANSFORMING LIVES

Did you know, we can use CGM not only to monitor diabetics but also in non-diabetics. Let's have a peak into this amazing technology.

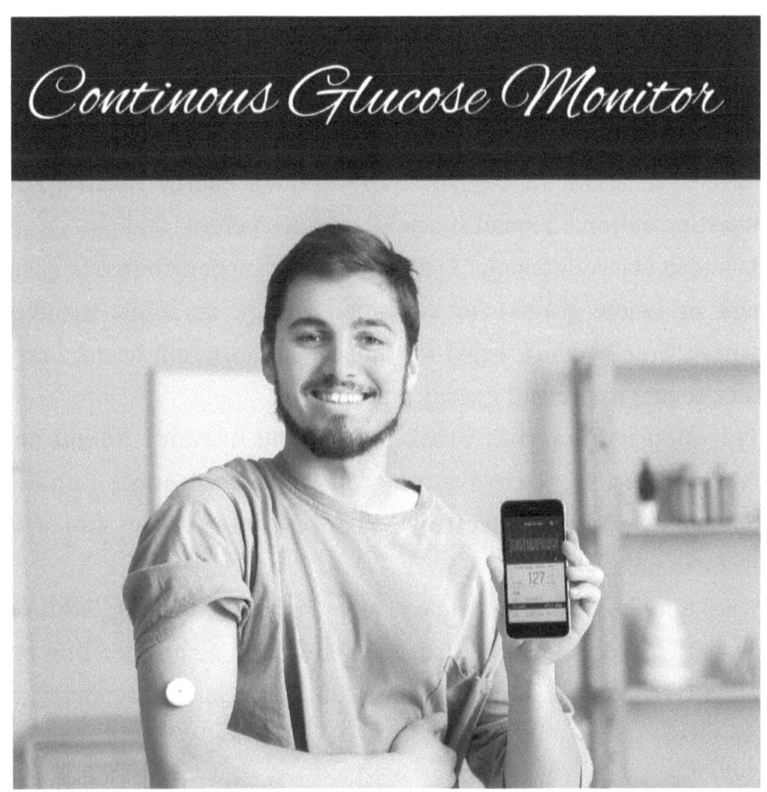

Optimizing Workout Performance with CGM & Millets – The Alamirap Approach

Post-COVID, fitness enthusiasts are **more aware of the importance of blood sugar stability** for **sustained energy, muscle growth, and fat loss**. By using **Continuous Glucose Monitoring (CGM), AlaMirap Nutrition** has helped athletes and gym-goers **fine-tune their pre and post-workout nutrition** for **peak performance and faster recovery**.

How CGM Helped Optimize Pre & Post-Workout Energy Levels

☑ **Problem:** Many fitness enthusiasts struggle with **energy crashes, poor endurance, or slow muscle recovery** due to **unbalanced blood sugar levels** before and after workouts.

☑ **Solution:** By tracking **real-time glucose data with CGM**, we identified the best **millet-based meal combinations** to provide **steady energy before workouts** and **faster glycogen replenishment post-workout**.

5 Key Evidence-Based Pointers for Pre-Workout Nutrition

1. Timing Matters: Consume a balanced meal 60–90 minutes before exercise to allow for digestion and optimal energy release. For fast-digesting options, a small snack 30 minutes before can help.
2. Balanced Macronutrients: Include complex carbohydrates (e.g., millets, oats, or whole grains) for sustained energy, moderate protein (e.g., paneer, Greek yogurt, eggs) for muscle support, and healthy fats (e.g., nuts, seeds) to prevent energy crashes.
3. Hydration is Essential: Drink 300–500ml of water 30–60 minutes before exercise. Dehydration can reduce strength, endurance, and focus. Adding electrolytes or coconut water can enhance performance.
4. Avoid Simple Sugars and Heavy Fats: High-GI foods (e.g., white bread, sweets) cause rapid blood sugar spikes and crashes, leading to early fatigue. Heavy fats slow digestion and may cause discomfort during exercise.

5. Caffeine for Performance Boost: 100–200mg of caffeine (from coffee or green tea) taken 30–45 minutes before a workout can enhance endurance, strength, and focus without causing energy crashes if combined with proper nutrition.

5 Best Millet-Based Pre-Workout Snacks

Millet-based curd rice is an excellent pre-workout snack, especially for those doing moderate-intensity workouts like yoga, brisk walking, strength training, or cardio. It gives you:

- Complex carbs from millet
- Good fats (if tempered with ghee or oil)
- Probiotics from curd
- Hydration and satiety without heaviness

Perfect for gut comfort, sustained energy, and anti-inflammatory support too.

Recipe 31 – Millet Curd Rice – Pre-Workout Snack (Serves 1)

Ingredients:

- Little Millet (Saamai) – ¼ cup
- Water – ¾ cup (to cook the millet)
- Curd (thick, homemade preferred) – ½ cup
- Grated cucumber – 1 tbsp (optional – cooling & hydrating)
- Grated carrot – 1 tbsp (optional – fibre + colour)
- Salt – to taste
- Ginger – ¼ tsp, finely grated
- Fresh coriander – 1 tsp, finely chopped

Tempering (optional but flavourful)

- Cold-pressed groundnut oil or ghee – ½ tsp
- Mustard seeds – ¼ tsp
- Cumin seeds – ¼ tsp
- Urad dal – ¼ tsp
- Hing (asafoetida) – a pinch
- Curry leaves – 4–5 leaves
- Green chilli – ¼, finely chopped (optional for light spice)

Preparation Steps

1. Cook the Millet
    - Rinse ¼ cup little millet well.
    - Cook in ¾ cup water on low heat until soft and fluffy (about 12–15 mins).
    - Let it cool slightly.
2. Prepare the Curd Mix
    - In a bowl, whisk the curd until smooth.
    - Add salt, grated ginger, cucumber, carrot, and coriander.
    - Once millet cools down (lukewarm or room temp), mix into the curd base.

3. Temper the Flavours
    - Heat oil or ghee in a small pan.
    - Add mustard, cumin, urad dal. Let them splutter.
    - Add hing, curry leaves, and green chilli (if using).
    - Pour over the curd rice mixture. Mix gently.
4. Rest for 5 minutes (optional but helps the flavours soak in).

    Best Time to Eat

    - 30–45 minutes before workout
    - Light, digestible, gives stable energy without bloating.

Pari's Super Tips:

- Add 1 tsp chia seeds or soaked flaxseeds for extra fibre and satiety.
- You can replace little millet with barnyard millet or kodo millet if preferred.
- For intense workouts, top with a few roasted peanuts or a boiled egg on the side.

Recipe 32 – Foxtail Millet & Nut Energy Balls

Ingredients:

- ½ cup foxtail millet flour
- ¼ cup dates (pitted & soaked)
- 2 tbsp peanut butter or almond butter
- 2 tbsp flaxseeds (omega-3 & fiber)
- 2 tbsp chopped almonds & cashews
- ½ tsp cinnamon powder
- 1 tsp honey or jaggery

How to Prepare:

1. Dry roast foxtail millet flour for 2 minutes.
2. Blend dates, nut butter, and honey into a smooth paste.
3. Mix with roasted millet flour, flaxseeds, and nuts.
4. Roll into small balls and refrigerate for 10 minutes before consuming.

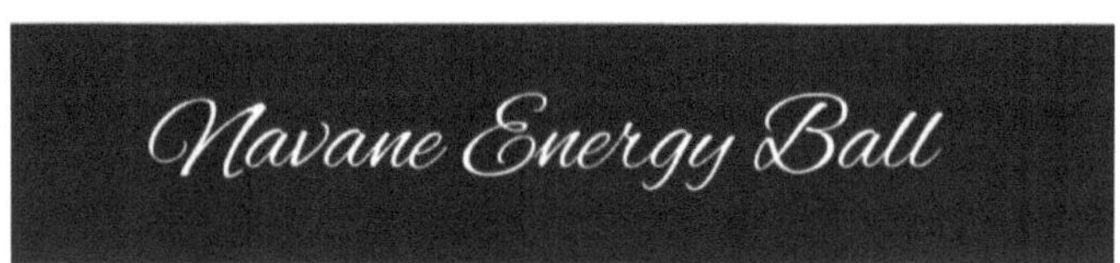

Recipe 33 – Pearl Millet Pancakes with Greek Yogurt & Honey

(For Balanced Carbs & Protein)

Ingredients:

- ½ cup bajra (pearl millet) flour
- 1 egg (for protein)
- ¼ cup Greek yogurt
- 1 tsp honey
- ¼ tsp baking soda
- ½ tsp cinnamon
- Water (as needed)

How to Prepare:

1. Mix bajra flour, egg, Greek yogurt, honey, baking soda, and cinnamon to form a batter.
2. Heat a pan and cook small pancakes until golden brown on both sides.
3. Serve with a drizzle of honey or nut butter.

Recipe 34 – Bajra Millet & Peanut Butter Toast (For Long-Lasting Energy)

Ingredients:

- 2 slices millet bread (or bajra/jowar roti)
- 1 tbsp peanut butter
- ½ banana (sliced)
- 1 tsp chia seeds or sesame seeds

How to Prepare:

1. Toast millet bread or roti until slightly crisp.
2. Spread peanut butter, add banana slices, and sprinkle chia or sesame seeds.
3. Enjoy a protein and fiber-packed snack.
4. **Jowar Porridge with Berries & Seeds *(For Slow-Release Carbs & Antioxidants)***

Ingredients:

- ½ cup jowar (sorghum) flour
- 1 cup low-fat milk or almond milk
- 1 tbsp chia or flaxseeds
- ¼ cup mixed berries (strawberries, blueberries)
- 1 tsp honey

How to Prepare:

1. Cook jowar flour with milk on low heat until thickened.
2. Stir in chia seeds and let it rest for 2 minutes.
3. Top with berries and honey before serving.

5 Key Evidence-Based Post-Workout Nutrition Pointers

1. The Golden Hour (30–60 Minutes Window): Post-workout, the body is in a high-absorption state, making this the best time to consume protein and carbohydrates for muscle repair and glycogen replenishment.
2. Protein for Muscle Recovery: Aim for 20–30g of protein to promote muscle repair and prevent breakdown. Best millet-based sources:
   - Millet & Greek Yogurt Smoothie
   - Millet Dosa with Paneer Filling
   - Bajra Roti with Dal & Curd
3. Carbs for Glycogen Replenishment: Choose complex carbs to restore muscle energy without spiking blood sugar. Best millet-based choices:
   - Foxtail Millet Porridge with Nuts
   - Barnyard Millet Khichdi with Ghee
   - Jowar Upma with Vegetables
4. Electrolyte & Hydration Balance: Exercise depletes sodium, potassium, and magnesium, which are essential for preventing cramps and fatigue.
   - Drink coconut water or lemon-millet water to replenish electrolytes.
   - Add sesame seeds, nuts, or dark leafy greens to your meal for magnesium.
5. Healthy Fats for Hormonal Recovery: Good fats help absorb fat-soluble vitamins and support hormone production. Include nuts, seeds, ghee, or avocado in your post-workout meal to sustain energy and aid recovery.

By combining millets with protein, carbs, and healthy fats, AlaMirap Nutrition ensures faster muscle recovery, sustained energy, and balanced hormones post-workout.

Millet-Based Post-Workout Salads for Muscle Recovery & Energy

These high-protein, fiber-rich millet salads are perfect for muscle repair, glycogen replenishment, and reducing inflammation after a workout.

Recipe 35 – Foxtail Millet & Chickpea Power Salad

Best for: Muscle recovery, protein synthesis, and gut health.

Ingredients:

- ½ cup cooked foxtail millet
- ½ cup boiled chickpeas (rich in protein & fiber)
- ½ cup cucumber & cherry tomatoes, chopped
- ¼ cup red bell pepper, diced (vitamin C for better recovery)
- 1 tbsp pumpkin seeds (magnesium for muscle relaxation)
- 1 tbsp olive oil
- 1 tsp lemon juice
- ½ tsp black pepper & salt
- 1 tbsp chopped coriander or mint

How to Prepare:

1. Mix cooked millet, chickpeas, and vegetables in a bowl.
2. Drizzle with olive oil, lemon juice, black pepper, and salt.
3. Toss well and top with pumpkin seeds and coriander.

☑ Why it works: High in protein, fiber, and healthy fats, ensuring steady energy and muscle recovery.

Recipe 36 – Bajra (Pearl Millet) & Paneer Protein Salad

Best for: Lean muscle building and post-workout electrolyte balance.

Ingredients:

- ½ cup cooked bajra (pearl millet)
- ½ cup grilled paneer, cubed (rich in casein protein for slow muscle repair)
- ¼ cup steamed spinach (iron & magnesium for better muscle function)
- ¼ cup chopped carrots & onions
- 1 tbsp flaxseeds or sesame seeds
- 1 tbsp Greek yogurt dressing (Greek yogurt + garlic + lemon juice + salt)
- ½ tsp black pepper

How to Prepare:

1. Grill paneer cubes on a non-stick pan until golden brown.
2. Toss cooked bajra, grilled paneer, spinach, carrots, and onions in a bowl.
3. Mix with Greek yogurt dressing, black pepper, and flaxseeds.

☑ Why it works: Provides slow-digesting carbs, protein, and essential minerals, keeping you full and aiding recovery.

Recipe 37 – Masala Ragi Gangi (Finger Millet Porridge) – Post-Workout Power Bowl

A warm, savoury, and easy-to-digest finger millet-based recipe perfect for recovery. Ragi (finger millet) is rich in calcium, iron, amino acids, and complex carbs – making it ideal for muscle recovery, gut health, and replenishing energy post workout.

Ingredients (Serves 1)

- Ragi flour (finger millet flour) – 2 tablespoons
- Water – 1½ cups
- Coconut milk or diluted curd – 2 tablespoons *(optional, adds creaminess & electrolytes)*
- Ghee – ½ teaspoon

Masala Mix:

- Cumin seeds – ¼ teaspoon
- Finely chopped ginger – ½ teaspoon
- Green chilli – ¼, finely chopped *(optional)*
- Curry leaves – 4–5 leaves
- Grated coconut – 1 tablespoon
- Salt – to taste
- Asafoetida (hing) – a pinch
- Fresh coriander – chopped, for garnish

Step-by-Step Preparation

Step 1: Mix Ragi Slurry

- In a small bowl, mix 2 tbsp ragi flour with ¼ cup water.
- Stir well to form a lump-free slurry. Set aside.

Step 2: Heat & Boil

- In a saucepan, bring 1¼ cups water to a gentle boil.
- Add salt, grated ginger, and hing.
- Once boiling, slowly pour in the ragi slurry, stirring continuously to avoid lumps.

Step 3: Cook the Ragi

- Cook on low flame for 6–8 minutes, stirring constantly.
- The mixture will thicken and turn glossy.
- Turn off the heat and let it rest for 2 minutes.

Step 4: Temper the Masala

- In a small pan, heat ½ tsp ghee.
- Add cumin seeds, green chilli, and curry leaves. Let them splutter.
- Add grated coconut and sauté for 30 seconds.

Step 5: Assemble

- Pour the tempering into the ragi mixture.
- Stir in 2 tbsp coconut milk or diluted curd if using.
- Garnish with fresh coriander.

When to Consume

- Ideal within 30–60 minutes post workout
- Helps refuel glycogen, rehydrate, and support muscle recovery

Pari's Super Tips:

- Add 1 tsp roasted sesame seeds for added calcium.
- If taken after strength training, pair with a boiled egg or handful of soaked almonds.
- Can be made sweeter with jaggery and cardamom for variation.

Recipe 38 – Millet Chicken Recovery Soup

Protein-rich, anti-inflammatory, and easy on the gut – perfect post-workout snack.

Ingredients (Serves 2)

- Boneless chicken – 100g (cut into small cubes or shredded)
- Cooked foxtail millet (or little millet) – ½ cup
- Carrot – ¼ cup (chopped)
- Spinach or amaranth leaves – ½ cup (shredded)
- Ginger – 1 tsp (finely chopped)
- Garlic – 2 cloves (crushed)
- Pepper powder – ½ tsp (freshly ground)
- Turmeric powder – ¼ tsp
- Cumin seeds – ½ tsp
- Ghee or cold-pressed coconut oil – 1 tsp
- Rock salt – to taste
- Water or homemade chicken stock – 2½ to 3 cups

Step-by-Step Preparation

1. Cook the Chicken
    - In a pot, add a few drops of ghee or oil.
    - Sauté ginger, garlic, and cumin till fragrant.
    - Add chicken pieces, sprinkle salt, turmeric, and pepper.
    - Sear lightly for 2 minutes.
2. Add Veggies & Water
    - Add carrots and 2.5 to 3 cups water (or stock).
    - Bring to a boil, then reduce to simmer for 10 minutes or until chicken is cooked.
3. Add Cooked Millet
    - Add ½ cup cooked foxtail millet to the soup.
    - Stir well and let it simmer for another 5 minutes to absorb flavours.

4. Finish with Greens
    - Add shredded spinach or amaranth leaves.
    - Simmer for 2 minutes, then switch off the flame.
5. Garnish & Serve
    - Sprinkle fresh pepper, a few drops of ghee, and coriander leaves if desired.
    - Serve warm.

Why This Works for Post-Workout

- Chicken = lean protein for muscle repair
- Millet = slow-release carbs + fibre
- Ginger, turmeric, cumin = anti-inflammatory & digestive
- Spinach = iron + micronutrients
- Warm broth = rehydration and gut comfort

Pari's Super Tips:

Add a few drops of lemon juice after cooking to improve iron absorption.

For extra calories post intense workouts, add 1 tsp ghee while serving.

5 Post-Workout Millet-Based Snacks

1. Barnyard Millet & Chicken Stir-Fry
2. Ragi & Greek Yogurt Protein Bowl
3. Jowar & Tofu Scramble on Millet Toast
4. Foxtail Millet & Coconut Smoothie
5. Bajra & Sprout Salad with Lemon Dressing

Please feel free to experiment which combination suits you the best.

There is no one rule fits all. We are all in the hunt for better health and better nutrition.

The Bottom Line:

✓ Millets are **excellent for sustained energy, muscle strength, and endurance**.

✓ Pair millets with **protein sources** for **optimal muscle recovery**.

✓ **Hydrate well** & **balance meals** with healthy fats & micronutrients.

📌 *Millets are a natural, nutrient-dense alternative to refined grains—making them a **powerful fuel** for athletes & bodybuilders!*

SUCCESS STORY – 9

Raja's Triathlon Transformation – How CGM & Millets Helped Him Win

Raja always considered himself fit. As a 32-year-old endurance athlete from Chennai, he had completed multiple marathons and cycling events. But when he set his sights on his first triathlon—a gruelling combination of swimming, cycling, and running—he realized his usual training wasn't enough.

Despite his intense workouts, Raja struggled with fatigue, inconsistent energy levels, and slow recovery. Some days, he felt strong and fast; other days, his muscles felt heavy, and his endurance dipped. No matter how much he trained, he couldn't pinpoint what was holding him back.

That's when he turned to AlaMirap Nutrition for a scientific approach to his diet.

The Turning Point: Understanding His Body with CGM

AlaMirap's experts suggested Continuous Glucose Monitoring (CGM) to track how his body reacted to different foods before, during, and after workouts. Raja was skeptical at first—he thought CGM was only for diabetics—but once he started wearing the tiny sensor, the data shocked him.

What CGM Revealed:

- His morning bowl of oats & honey caused a glucose spike, leading to an energy crash during training.
- His post-workout meals lacked the right carbs and proteins, slowing his muscle recovery.
- Eating refined carbs before a workout made his body burn sugar too quickly, leaving him exhausted mid-run.

The patterns were clear—his diet wasn't supporting his training. He wasn't eating wrong, but he wasn't eating right for his body.

That's when AlaMirap introduced Millet-Based Endurance Nutrition into his plan.

The 3-Month Transformation: Millets as Performance Fuel

Raja's customized meal plan focused on slow-digesting complex carbs, protein-packed meals, and better recovery foods.

Month 1: Fixing Energy Crashes

- Oats were replaced with Ragi & Almond Smoothies – Slower energy release, no mid-race fatigue.
- Foxtail Millet & Sweet Potato Pre-Workout Meal – Improved stamina without glucose spikes.

Results: Raja noticed longer-lasting energy, especially in his cycling sessions.

Month 2: Enhancing Recovery

- Jowar & Paneer Stir-Fry after workouts for protein & muscle repair.
- Barnyard Millet & Chicken Bowl – Faster glycogen replenishment, reduced muscle soreness.

Results: Quicker recovery, no more heavy legs before training.

Month 3: Race Simulation & Fine-Tuning

- Millet & Peanut Butter Energy Balls for Mid-Race Fuel – No energy dips.
- Hydration optimized with Coconut Water & Electrolytes.

Results: Raja completed his first full-distance triathlon simulation with steady energy levels.

Race Day: A Game-Changer

After 3 months of CGM-based nutrition and millet-powered fuelling, Raja was a different athlete. His energy was consistent, his endurance was stronger than ever, and his recovery faster.

During the triathlon, he followed his new nutrition strategy—no sudden crashes, no fatigue, just pure focus and performance. He shaved off 20 minutes from his expected finishing time and completed the race feeling stronger than ever.

As he crossed the finish line, exhausted but victorious, Raja realized this wasn't just about one race. It was about understanding his body, fuelling it right, and performing at his best—every single day.

SUCCESS STORY - 10

Nidhi's Journey: How Millets Transformed Her Yoga Practice in Just One Month

At 66, **Nidhi** was full of life. A retired teacher and homemaker from **Pune**, she had recently started **yoga classes** to stay active. But despite her enthusiasm, she felt **tired too quickly, struggled to hold poses, and lacked the stamina to complete an hour-long session**.

She had **no major health issues**—her reports were normal, but she constantly felt **low on energy**. After trying different foods and supplements with little success, she decided to take a natural approach. That's when she turned to **AlaMirap Nutrition** for guidance.

The Millet-Powered Plan: Natural Energy Without Stimulants

Nidhi's nutritionist at **AlaMirap** realized that **her meals weren't supporting her yoga practice**. She was eating **light but not balanced**, leading to **quick energy dips**. The solution? **Millet-based pre- and post-yoga nutrition.**

Pre-Yoga: Fueling Energy Without Heaviness

Before yoga, Nidhi needed something **light yet sustaining**, to prevent fatigue without feeling too full.

- ✓ **What She Was Eating Before:** Just tea and biscuits—leading to an energy crash mid-session.
- ✓ **New Pre-Yoga Meal: Foxtail Millet & Almond Smoothie** – A blend of foxtail millet, soaked almonds, dates, and warm milk.

Results in Week 1: She felt **more stable, no lightheadedness**, and **better flexibility in poses.**

Post-Yoga: Recovery Without Sluggishness

After yoga, her body needed **protein and nutrients** to avoid post-session exhaustion.

- ✓ **What She Was Eating Before:** Just fruit or a simple meal, but **no protein or healthy fats.**
- ✓ **New Post-Yoga Meal: Jowar & Paneer Stir-Fry** – A warm, protein-rich meal with jowar, lightly sautéed paneer, and vegetables.

Results by Week 3: She felt **energized after yoga instead of drained** and could now **hold poses longer with better strength.**

One Month Later: A Noticeable Difference

By the end of **four weeks**, Nidhi noticed:

- ✓ **Consistent energy levels throughout the day**
- ✓ **Improved focus & balance in yoga**
- ✓ **No more mid-morning fatigue or cravings**
- ✓ **Feeling lighter but stronger**

Her journey wasn't about **losing weight or fixing health issues**—it was about **feeling more alive, more capable, and more in control of her energy.**

Now, every morning, she enjoys her **millet smoothie before yoga** and **a nourishing post-yoga meal**, knowing that her **body is getting exactly what it needs to thrive.**

5 Simple Psychological Pointers for Better Health for Housewives

1. Prioritize Yourself Without Guilt – Taking care of your family is important, but your health comes first. A healthy, happy you means a stronger family. Give yourself permission to rest, eat well, and exercise without feeling guilty.
2. Practice Mindful Eating – Avoid eating in a rush or while multitasking. Sit down, chew slowly, and enjoy your meals. This improves digestion, prevents overeating, and allows you to connect with your food.
3. Create a Positive Kitchen Environment – Treat your kitchen as a healing space, not just a place of duty. Keep it clean, organized, and filled with fresh, wholesome ingredients that make you excited to cook and eat well.
4. Listen to Your Body's Signals – Instead of ignoring fatigue, cravings, or mood swings, recognize them as signs your body is giving you. Adjust your diet, hydration, and rest accordingly to maintain balance.
5. Stay Connected & Engage in Joyful Movement – Health isn't just about food. Walking, yoga, dancing, or even gardening can uplift your mood and energy. Social connections, even casual conversations, help reduce stress and boost emotional well-being.

By making small yet intentional changes, any homemaker can feel more energetic, emotionally balanced, and in control of her well-being.

Chapter 8

LIFESTYLE AND MEAL PLANNING

"A goal without a plan is just a wish." – Antoine de Saint-Exupéry

True **healthy living** goes beyond just the food on our plate—it's about how we weave those choices into our daily routines. In the whirlwind of life, a well-planned approach to meals and mindful habits can be the difference between feeling **energized and in control** or **overwhelmed and exhausted.**

This chapter will guide you in:

- **Designing a lifestyle that nurtures long-term well-being**
- **Building a sustainable, enjoyable relationship with food**
- **Harnessing the power of millets to fuel your body with strength and vitality**

A thoughtful approach to food and daily habits doesn't just improve health—it transforms the way we live, one mindful choice at a time.

Why Lifestyle Changes & Meal Planning Matter

Between work, family responsibilities, and social commitments, it's easy to slip into habits of convenience. But health doesn't happen by accident—it requires intention and planning.

The Benefits of a Planned Lifestyle

✓ **Saves Time & Reduces Stress** – No more last-minute meal scrambles or resorting to unhealthy takeout.

✓ **Improves Nutrition** – Ensures meals are balanced and nutrient-rich. Millets, with their high fibre, vitamins, and minerals, play a crucial role here.

✓ **Encourages Portion Control** – Planned meals prevent mindless snacking and help maintain a healthy calorie balance.

✓ **Boosts Mental Well-being** – Having a structured routine reduces decision fatigue, bringing a sense of control and stability.

By taking the time to plan meals and structure your day, you're not just feeding your body—you're nurturing your mind.

7-days / Weekly Meal Plan with Millet Recipes

Here's a 7-day meal plan incorporating delicious and easy millet-based recipes to keep you energised and satisfied.

Day 1

- Breakfast: Ragi Banana Pancakes with Greek yogurt & berries
- Mid-Morning Snack: Popped Jowar Trail Mix
- Lunch: Foxtail Millet Salad with grilled chicken & lemon dressing
- Afternoon Snack: Millet Energy Ball (pearl millet, dates, almonds)
- Dinner: Barnyard Millet & Vegetable Soup

Day 2

- Breakfast: Little Millet Porridge with almond milk & fruits
- Mid-Morning Snack: 1 small apple + 10 almonds
- Lunch: Kodo Millet "Fried Rice" with tofu, peas & carrots
- Afternoon Snack: Jowar Masala Puffs + Green Tea
- Dinner: Proso Millet Khichdi with lentils & sautéed spinach

Day 3

- Breakfast: Ragi Malt Drink with jaggery & cardamom
- Mid-Morning Snack: Bajra Veggie Crackers with hummus
- Lunch: Little Millet Tacos with beans, veggies & yogurt dressing
- Afternoon Snack: Fresh fruit salad
- Dinner: Foxtail Millet & Paneer Curry + cucumber raita

Day 4

- Breakfast: Foxtail Millet Upma with mixed vegetables & curry leaves
- Mid-Morning Snack: Ragi Laddoo (made with jaggery & nuts)
- Lunch: Jowar Vegetable Stir-Fry with bell peppers, carrots & tofu
- Afternoon Snack: Popped Bajra Mix with peanuts & dry fruits
- Dinner: Little Millet Pulao with mixed veggies & cucumber raita

Day 5

- Breakfast: Ragi Banana Smoothie with almond milk & chia seeds
- Mid-Morning Snack: Bajra Veggie Crackers with homemade yogurt dip
- Lunch: Barnyard Millet Salad Bowl with leafy greens, chickpeas, cucumber & lemon vinaigrette
- Afternoon Snack: Millet Energy Ball (dates, nuts & seeds)
- Dinner: Proso Millet Soup with spinach, carrots & a light vegetable broth

Day 6

- Breakfast: Little Millet Porridge with coconut milk, dates & almonds
- Mid-Morning Snack: Roasted Jowar Puffs with herbs & spices
- Lunch: Foxtail Millet Buddha Bowl with roasted veggies & tahini dressing
- Afternoon Snack: Ragi Murukku (air-fried or baked) with herbal tea
- Dinner: Kodo Millet & Lentil Khichdi with turmeric & sautéed greens

Day 7

- Breakfast: Bajra Pancakes with honey & fresh fruits
- Mid-Morning Snack: Fruit Salad with chia seeds
- Lunch: Little Millet Tacos filled with grilled veggies, beans & yogurt dressing
- Afternoon Snack: Millet & Nut Trail Mix
- Dinner: Foxtail Millet Veggie Soup with a side of mixed greens salad

Why This Meal Plan Works

☑ Balanced & Nutritious – Includes protein, fibre, healthy fats & micronutrients in every meal.

☑ Keeps You Full & Energised – Millets provide sustained energy & keep cravings in check.

☑ Easy to Prepare & Enjoy – Simple, flavourful meals with variety & flexibility.

☑ **Gut-Friendly & Helps in hormonal balance.

5 Practical Tips for Meal Prepping & Storage

Meal prepping saves time, reduces stress, and keeps healthy choices accessible. Here's how to make the process easy:

1. Plan Your Menu for the Week
   - ✓ Choose recipes with common ingredients to simplify prep.
   - ✓ Example: If making Millet Khichdi, use the same veggies for Millet Soup & Cutlets.
2. Cook Millets in Batches
   - ✓ Cook ragi, foxtail millet, or barnyard millet at the start of the week.
   - ✓ Store in airtight containers (lasts 5 days in the fridge).
   - ✓ Use for salads, porridges, or main dishes throughout the week.
3. Prep Ingredients in Advance
   - ✓ Chop vegetables, boil lentils, & marinate proteins ahead of time.
   - ✓ Store in separate containers for easy mixing.
4. Make Snack Packs
   - ✓ Pre-portion Jowar Mix, Millet Energy Balls & Bajra Crackers for grab-and-go snacks.
5. Store Smartly
   - ✓ Use clear containers to easily see what you have.
   - ✓ Label & date items to track freshness.
   - ✓ Freeze portions of cooked millets for future meals.

Balancing Nutrition Throughout the Day

A balanced diet involves distributing nutrients properly across meals.

- ✓ Breakfast – Focus on complex carbs (millets), protein (yogurt, nuts, or eggs), & healthy fats to stay full longer.
- ✓ Lunch – A balanced plate: millets, veggies, protein (chicken, tofu, lentils), & a small serving of healthy fat (olive oil, avocado).
- ✓ Dinner – Keep it light yet filling. Millet soups, khichdis, or stir-fries are great options.

✓ Snacks – Choose high-fibre, nutrient-rich options like Millet Energy Balls, Jowar Mix, or fresh fruits with nuts.

Meal Prepping Tips for Busy Lifestyles

Meal prepping is a game-changer for maintaining a healthy lifestyle. Setting aside just a few hours a week can help you save time, reduce stress, and always have nutritious options ready. Here's how to make meal prepping easy and effective:

1. Choose Your Prep Day(s)
   - ✓ Select one or two days a week to prepare meals. Many find Sundays & Wednesdays work best.
   - ✓ Dedicate 2–3 hours on these days for cooking & storing meals.
2. Plan Your Menu & Make a Shopping List
   - ✓ Use a meal plan (like the one we covered) to create a weekly menu.
   - ✓ Write a shopping list and organise it by categories (vegetables, grains, proteins, snacks) to save time & avoid impulse purchases.
3. Cook Millets in Bulk
   - ✓ Cook large batches of Ragi, Foxtail Millet, Barnyard Millet & Little Millet—they stay fresh for up to 5 days in the fridge.
   - ✓ Cook them plain (without seasoning) so they can be used flexibly in salads, porridges, or main dishes.
   - ✓ Store in airtight containers or portion them into smaller servings for easy access.

4. Prepare Mix-and-Match Components
   - ✓ Chop Vegetables: Wash & dice carrots, bell peppers, cucumbers, leafy greens—store them separately for easy meal assembly.
   - ✓ Cook Proteins: Pre-cook grilled chicken, paneer, tofu, or boiled chickpeas to make meal prep quicker.
   - ✓ Make Sauces & Dressings: Prepare yogurt dip, lemon vinaigrette, or peanut dressing—store in glass jars for freshness.
5. Assemble Ready-to-Eat Meals
   - ✓ Salad Jars: Layer dressing at the bottom & leafy greens on top to keep them fresh.
   - ✓ Pre-Portion Snacks: Store Millet Energy Balls, Bajra Crackers, or Popped Jowar Mix in easy-to-grab containers.
   - ✓ Ready Meals: Prepare Millet Buddha Bowls, Millet Stir-Fries, or Khichdi in containers that can go from fridge to microwave.
6. Store Smart & Safe
   - ✓ Use clear, airtight containers so you can easily see what you have.
   - ✓ Label & date containers to track freshness and prevent food waste.
   - ✓ Store in the fridge for up to 5 days or freeze for longer storage.
   - ✓ Use stackable containers to save space & keep your fridge organised.

Why Meal Prepping Works:

- ☑ Saves time—No more last-minute cooking stress!
- ☑ Encourages healthy eating—You have nutritious meals ready when hunger strikes.
- ☑ Reduces food waste—Everything is planned & stored properly.
- ☑ Keeps you consistent—When healthy food is convenient, you're more likely to stick to your goals!

A little preparation goes a long way in building a sustainable, stress-free healthy lifestyle!

Balancing Nutrition Throughout the Day

1. Start Your Day Right with Breakfast
   - Breakfast jumpstarts metabolism, fuels your body, and sets the tone for the day. A balanced breakfast should include complex carbs, protein, and healthy fats.
   - Examples:
     - ✓ Ragi Banana Smoothie Bowl – Ragi flour, banana, Greek yogurt, chia seeds & nuts
     - ✓ Foxtail Millet Upma – Foxtail millet with mixed veggies & peanuts for protein
     - ✓ Bajra Pancakes – Bajra flour with yogurt & fruits
2. Energise with a Balanced Lunch
   - Lunch should provide sustained energy without causing an afternoon slump. Include complex carbs, lean protein, and healthy fats.
   - Examples:
     - ✓ Little Millet Salad Bowl – Little millet, chickpeas, leafy greens, cucumber & lemon vinaigrette
     - ✓ Foxtail Millet Buddha Bowl – Roasted veggies, tofu, foxtail millet & tahini dressing
     - ✓ Barnyard Millet Khichdi – Barnyard millet with moong dal, turmeric & spinach
3. Light and Nutritious Dinner
   - Dinner should be light and easy to digest to promote restful sleep. Millets combined with veggies and lean protein make the perfect meal.
   - Examples:
     - ✓ Proso Millet Soup – Proso millet, vegetable broth, spinach & carrots
     - ✓ Jowar Vegetable Stir-Fry – Jowar with mixed veggies & tofu
     - ✓ Kodo Millet & Lentil Khichdi – Kodo millet, lentils & a side of cucumber raita

4. Smart Snacking to Keep You Full and Energised
    - Snacks help maintain energy levels and prevent overeating at meals. Choose high-fibre, nutrient-rich options.
    - Examples:
        - ✓ Millet Energy Balls – Pearl millet flour, dates & nuts
        - ✓ Popped Jowar Trail Mix – Jowar puffs, almonds, pumpkin seeds & dried fruits
        - ✓ Ragi Laddoos – Ragi flour, jaggery & nuts for a sweet, healthy treat

Motivational Strategies for Staying Consistent

Staying consistent with healthy habits can be challenging, but these strategies keep you on track:

1. Set Realistic Goals
    - ✓ Break down big goals into small, manageable steps.
    - ✓ Example: Instead of "I'll eat healthy every day," try "I'll include millets in one meal daily."
2. Track Your Progress
    - ✓ Keep a journal or use an app to track meals, mood & energy levels.
    - ✓ Helps you see how food choices impact well-being.
3. Celebrate Small Wins
    - ✓ Prepped all meals this week? Great! Treat yourself to a relaxing bath or movie night.
4. Stay Flexible
    - ✓ Missed a meal prep day or had an unplanned treat? No stress! Just get back on track with your next meal.

Motivational Boost: Consistency Over Perfection

One of the biggest challenges in maintaining a healthy lifestyle is the pressure to be perfect. But progress, not perfection, is the goal.

"Success is the sum of small efforts, repeated day in and day out." – Robert Collier

"You don't have to be perfect to be amazing."

"A small step forward is still progress. Keep going!"

Final Thought: You Are in Control of Your Health!

Every millet meal, mindful moment, and step toward a balanced lifestyle is a victory worth celebrating. Your journey matters, and every small change adds up.

📌 *Looking for a custom meal plan? Let AlaMirap Nutrition help you create a lifestyle that nourishes and empowers you!*

Chapter 8

BREAKFAST BOOSTERS

"Eat breakfast like a king, lunch like a prince, dinner like a pauper."
– Adelle Davis

A healthy breakfast is important for everyone, not just kids. It sets the tone for the day by providing essential nutrients and energy. Here's why it matters for different age groups:

For Kids

1. **Boosts Brain Function** – Helps with concentration, memory, and learning.
2. **Provides Energy** – Fuels their growing bodies for physical activities.
3. **Prevents Cravings** – Reduces the urge for junk food later in the day.
4. **Supports Growth** – Essential vitamins and minerals aid in development.
5. **Regulates Mood** – A nutritious start prevents irritability and tiredness.

For Mothers & Fathers

1. **Maintains Energy Levels** – Helps parents keep up with their daily responsibilities.
2. **Supports Metabolism** – A good breakfast kickstarts digestion and keeps weight in check.
3. **Reduces Stress** – Eating well balances blood sugar, preventing mood swings.
4. **Boosts Productivity** – A sharp mind leads to better decision-making at work and home.

For Grandparents

1. **Improves Bone Health** – Calcium and vitamin D from foods like millets, dairy, and nuts support bone strength.
2. **Enhances Digestion** – Fiber-rich breakfasts (like fruits and whole grains) aid gut health.
3. **Manages Blood Sugar** – A well-balanced breakfast stabilizes glucose levels, reducing diabetes risks.
4. **Keeps Muscles Strong** – Protein-rich meals prevent muscle loss with age.

A power-packed breakfast is the secret to a better day!

Recipe 39 – Millet Dosa Breakfast Combo (South Indian Style)

Main Dish: Multi-Millet Dosa

Ingredients (Makes ~6 dosas)

- Foxtail millet (thinai) – ½ cup
- Little millet (saamai) – ¼ cup
- Urad dal – ¼ cup
- Fenugreek seeds – ½ tsp
- Poha (flattened rice) – 2 tbsp (optional – for softness)
- Salt – to taste

Method:

1. Soak millets, urad dal, and fenugreek seeds for 5–6 hours.
2. Blend to a smooth batter with poha. Ferment overnight.
3. Add salt and make dosas on a hot tawa. Crisp edges, soft centre.

Side 1: Curry Leaf & Coconut Chutney

- Fresh coconut – ½ cup
- Curry leaves – 10–12
- Green chilli – 1
- Ginger – ½ inch
- Roasted chana dal – 2 tbsp
- Salt & water – as needed
- Blend to a smooth paste. Temper with mustard, urad dal, curry leaves.

Side 2: Horsegram (Kulith) Sambar *(Protein-packed & anti-inflammatory)*

- Cooked toor dal + horsegram
- Add tamarind water, sambar powder, tomatoes, shallots
- Simmer & temper with mustard, red chilli, and hing.

Optional Add-On: Spiced Millet Kanji Shot

- Make a small shot glass portion of fermented ragi kanji with curry leaf & ginger tempering – drink before or with breakfast as a gut-health tonic.

Pari's Super Tips:

- Rotate millets: Try barnyard or kodo millet next week.
- Add moringa leaves to the dosa batter for extra iron.
- Use cold-pressed oil or ghee for crisp dosas.

Recipe 40 – Pearl Millet Upma

Savoury Breakfast Packed with Fibre and Flavour

This Pearl Millet Upma is a perfect way to start the day with a warm, nutritious breakfast. Packed with fibre and protein, it's a filling dish that keeps you energised for hours.

Ingredients:

- Pearl Millet (Bajra): 1 cup (soaked and boiled)
- Mixed Vegetables: 1/2 cup (carrots, beans, peas)
- Onion: 1 (finely chopped)
- Mustard Seeds: 1 teaspoon
- Cumin Seeds: 1 teaspoon
- Urad Dal: 1 teaspoon
- Turmeric Powder: 1/2 teaspoon
- Coriander Powder: 1 teaspoon
- Curry Leaves: A few
- Oil: 2 tablespoons
- Salt: To taste
- Lemon Juice: A few drops
- Fresh Coriander Leaves: For garnish

Method:

1. Tempering:
    - Heat oil in a pan.
    - Add mustard seeds, cumin seeds, urad dal, and curry leaves.

    Let them splutter.
2. Sauté the Vegetables:
    - Add chopped onions and sauté until translucent.
    - Add turmeric powder, coriander powder, and salt. Mix well.
    - Add the mixed vegetables and cook until slightly tender.

3. Combine with Pearl Millet:
   - Add the soaked and boiled pearl millet to the pan.
   - Mix well and cook for 3–4 minutes to allow the flavours to blend.
4. Finishing Touch:
   - Squeeze some lemon juice for a tangy twist.
   - Garnish with freshly chopped coriander leaves.

Health Benefits:

- High in Fibre: Aids in digestion and keeps you full longer.
- Diabetic-Friendly: Low glycaemic index helps in controlling blood sugar levels.
- Rich in Iron and Magnesium: Boosts energy and supports muscle function.

Recipe 41 – Finger millet/Ragi Pancakes

Healthy Sweet Pancakes with a Protein Boost

Ingredients:

- Ragi Flour (Finger Millet): 1 cup
- Whole Wheat Flour: 1/2 cup (optional for fluffier pancakes)
- Jaggery Powder: 1/4 cup (or as per taste)
- Cardamom Powder: 1/2 teaspoon
- Milk (or Plant-Based Milk): 1 cup
- Banana: 1 (mashed)
- Baking Powder: 1 teaspoon
- Ghee or Oil: For cooking
- Honey and Fresh Fruits: For serving

Method:

1. Prepare the Batter:
    - In a bowl, mix Ragi flour, whole wheat flour, jaggery powder, cardamom powder, and baking powder.
    - Add milk gradually to make a smooth batter.
    - Mix in the mashed banana for natural sweetness.
2. Cook the Pancakes:
    - Heat a non-stick pan and lightly grease it with ghee or oil.
    - Pour a ladleful of batter and spread gently to form a pancake.
    - Cook on medium flame until bubbles appear, then flip and cook the other side.
3. Serve:
    - Stack the pancakes, drizzle with honey, and garnish with fresh fruits

Recipe 42 - Foxtail Millet Idli

Light and Fluffy Idlis Packed with Protein

Foxtail Millet Idli is a nutritious and delicious breakfast option. These light and fluffy idlis are gluten-free and rich in protein, making them perfect for a healthy start to the day.

They are easy to digest and pair beautifully with coconut chutney and sambar.

Ingredients:

- Foxtail Millet: 2 cups
- Urad Dal: 1 cup
- Fenugreek Seeds (Methi): 1 teaspoon
- Salt: To taste
- Water: As needed for soaking and grinding

Method:

1. Soak and Grind:
    - Soak the foxtail millet, urad dal, and fenugreek seeds separately for 6 hours.
    - Drain the water and grind the urad dal to a smooth, fluffy batter using a little water.
    - Grind the foxtail millet to a slightly coarse batter.
    - Mix both batters together, add salt, and leave it to ferment overnight.
2. Steam the Idlis:
    - Grease the idli plates with oil.
    - Pour the fermented batter into the idli moulds.
    - Steam for 10–12 minutes or until the idlis are cooked through.
3. Serve:
    - Serve hot with coconut chutney and sambar for a complete, nutritious breakfast.

Did You Know?

In **2024**, a food delivery app conducted a nationwide survey and revealed that **Idli** is the most preferred breakfast choice in India. Here are the key findings:

Survey Highlights

- **Idli was the top choice** across multiple cities, beating parathas, dosas, and poha.
- **Health-conscious eating habits** played a significant role in Idli's popularity.
- **Soft, easy to digest, and nutritious**, Idli appeals to all age groups.
- **Bangalore, Chennai, Hyderabad, and Mumbai** saw the highest orders for Idlis.
- **Working professionals and parents** preferred Idlis due to their light yet filling nature.

Why Idli Won?

1. **Healthy & Gut-Friendly** – Made from fermented rice and urad dal, it promotes digestion.
2. **Low in Calories** – Ideal for those looking to maintain weight.
3. **Versatile & Customizable** – Pairs well with sambar, chutneys, or even podi.
4. **Quick & Easy** – Convenient to prepare at home or order for delivery.
5. **Loved by All Ages** – Soft texture makes it perfect for kids, elders, and everyone in between.

Other Top Breakfast Choices (as per the survey)

- **Dosa** – Came in second place, especially loved in South India.
- **Paratha** – Popular in North India but seen as a heavier option.
- **Poha & Upma** – Ranked high for their lightness and quick preparation.

This survey confirms that while **new breakfast trends** come and go, **Idli remains timeless**, offering a **perfect balance of health, taste, and tradition**!

Recipe 43 – Little Millet Porridge (Saame Ganji)

Comforting and Nutritious Breakfast Bowl

This Little Millet Porridge is a comforting, warm breakfast option that is incredibly easy to make. It is rich in fibre and minerals, making it perfect for gut health and overall well being.

You can make it savoury or sweet, depending on your preference.

Ingredients:

For Savoury Porridge:

- Little Millet: 1 cup (washed and soaked for 2 hours)
- Water: 3 cups
- Salt: To taste
- Buttermilk: 1 cup
- Onion: 1 (finely chopped)
- Coriander Leaves: For garnish
- Curry Leaves: A few

For Sweet Porridge:

- Little Millet: 1 cup (washed and soaked for 2 hours)
- Water: 3 cups
- Jaggery: 1/4 cup (adjust to taste)
- Cardamom Powder: 1/2 teaspoon
- Coconut Milk: 1 cup
- Dry Fruits (Cashews, Raisins): For garnish

Method:

1. Cook the Little Millet:
    - In a thick-bottomed pan, add the soaked millet and water.
    - Cook on low flame until the millet is soft and mushy.

2. For Savoury Porridge:
    - Add salt and mix well.
    - Turn off the heat and add buttermilk.
    - Garnish with chopped onions, coriander leaves, and curry leaves.
    - Serve warm for a soothing breakfast.
3. For Sweet Porridge:
    - Once the millet is cooked, add jaggery and stir until it melts completely.
    - Add cardamom powder and mix well.
    - Turn off the heat and stir in the coconut milk.
    - Garnish with roasted dry fruits for added crunch.
    - Serve warm or chilled as per preference.

Health Benefits:

- Rich in Fibre: Aids digestion and promotes gut health.
- Nutrient-Dense: High in iron, magnesium, and antioxidants.
- Versatile and Customisable: Can be enjoyed both sweet and savoury.

Fuel Your Day the Right Way

Starting your day with a nutritious, balanced breakfast is one of the best ways to maintain energy levels and stay focused throughout the day. These millet-based breakfast recipes are not just delicious but also packed with essential nutrients that support overall health and well-being.

Millets are incredibly versatile and can be adapted to suit every palate – from savoury upmas and idlis to sweet pancakes and porridges. They are high in fibre, protein, and essential micronutrients, making them perfect for a balanced, wholesome breakfast.

Whether you are looking for a quick, on-the-go breakfast or a leisurely, comforting meal, millets offer a range of options that are not only healthy but also satisfying.

With these recipes, you can now make breakfast the most delightful part of your day.

"The first meal of the day is not just about feeding your body; it's about nourishing your mind and soul."

I hope these recipes inspire you to embrace millets as a staple in your morning routine. Start your day right and experience the difference it makes. Let's continue this millet journey in the next chapter, where we explore Power-Packed Lunches that are wholesome, delicious, and perfect for a busy lifestyle.

Stay energised. Stay healthy!

Chapter 10

POWER-PACKED LUNCHES AND TANTALIZING DINNER OPTIONS

Wholesome, Balanced Meals for a Busy Day

Lunch is not just about filling your stomach; it's about refuelling your body and mind for the rest of the day. A nutritious lunch boosts your energy levels, enhances focus, and keeps you satisfied without feeling heavy or sluggish.

Unfortunately, with our busy schedules, we often end up choosing convenience over health, settling for fast food or skipping lunch altogether. But what if you could prepare quick, delicious, and nutritious lunches using millets?

Millets are the perfect solution for power-packed lunches. They are rich in fibre, protein, vitamins, and minerals, making them ideal for a balanced meal. What's more, they are incredibly versatile and can be paired with a variety of vegetables, legumes, and spices to create flavourful dishes.

In this chapter, we'll explore five power-packed millet lunch recipes that are not only healthy but also delicious and easy to make.

Why Millets for Lunch?

- High in Fibre and Protein: Keeps you full longer and provides sustained energy.
- Low Glycaemic Index: Helps in maintaining stable blood sugar levels.
- Rich in Vitamins and Minerals: Boosts immunity and enhances overall health.
- Quick and Easy: Millets cook faster than rice or wheat and can be prepared in one pot.

"Let food be thy medicine and medicine be thy food." – Hippocrates

Recipe 44 – Kodo Millet Keerai Masiyal Rice

Fibre-rich, iron-packed, gut-friendly and deeply satisfying

Ingredients (Serves 2)

For the Millet:

- Kodo millet (Varagu) – ½ cup
- Water – 1½ cups
- Salt – to taste

For the Keerai Masiyal (Spinach Mash):

- Amaranth leaves / Arai keerai / Palak – 2 cups (chopped, tightly packed)
- Toor dal – ¼ cup (washed)
- Garlic – 3–4 cloves
- Green chilli – 1 (optional)
- Tomato – 1 small (chopped)
- Turmeric powder – ¼ tsp
- Salt – to taste
- Water – 1½ cups

Tempering:

- Gingelly oil / Ghee – 1 tbsp
- Mustard seeds – ½ tsp
- Urad dal – ½ tsp
- Cumin seeds – ½ tsp
- Dry red chillies – 1
- Hing – a pinch
- Curry leaves – 6–8

Step-by-Step Preparation

1. Cook the Millet:
    - Rinse kodo millet thoroughly.
    - Cook with 1.5 cups water and a pinch of salt.
    - Use pressure cooker (1–2 whistles) or open pot method until soft. Fluff and keep aside.
2. Prepare Keerai Masiyal:
    - In another pot or pressure cooker, add:
    - Toor dal, keerai, tomato, garlic, green chilli, turmeric, and water.
    - Pressure cook for 3 whistles, or boil until everything is soft.
    - Mash with a wooden masher or blend lightly for a coarse texture.
    - Add salt to taste.
3. Tempering:
    - Heat gingelly oil in a small pan.
    - Add mustard seeds, let them splutter.
    - Add urad dal, cumin, dry red chilli, hing, and curry leaves.
    - Pour over the keerai masiyal and mix well.
4. Serve:
    - Serve hot masiyal over kodo millet rice.
    - Drizzle with ghee for added richness.
    - Best paired with roasted appalam or pickle.

Pari's Super Tips:

- Add 1 tsp roasted sesame powder or crushed peanuts for extra calcium and taste.
- Rotate greens: Use moringa leaves, manathakkali, or sirukeerai weekly.
- For anaemia: Add beetroot or drumstick leaves to the masiyal.

Recipe 45 – Barnyard Millet Biryani

Aromatic and Flavourful One-Pot Meal

Who doesn't love a good biryani? This Millet Biryani is a healthier version of the traditional dish, using Barnyard Millet instead of rice. Barnyard Millet is rich in fibre and low in calories, making it a perfect choice for weight watchers. This one-pot meal is infused with aromatic spices and loaded with colourful vegetables, making it not only delicious but also visually appealing.

Ingredients:

- Barnyard Millet: 1 cup (washed and soaked for 30 minutes)
- Mixed Vegetables: 1 cup (carrots, beans, peas, and cauliflower)
- Onion: 1 (thinly sliced)
- Tomato: 1 (chopped)
- Ginger-Garlic Paste: 1 teaspoon
- Green Chillies: 2 (slit lengthwise)
- Bay Leaf: 1
- Cinnamon Stick: 1 small piece
- Cloves: 3
- Cardamom: 2
- Turmeric Powder: 1/2 teaspoon
- Red Chilli Powder: 1 teaspoon (adjust to taste)
- Biryani Masala Powder: 1 tablespoon
- Salt: To taste
- Ghee or Oil: 2 tablespoons

- Water: 2 cups
- Fresh Coriander and Mint Leaves: For garnish

Method:

1. Preparation: Wash and soak the barnyard millet for 30 minutes. Drain and set aside.
2. Tempering and Sautéing:
   - Heat ghee or oil in a pressure cooker.
   - Add bay leaf, cinnamon stick, cloves, and cardamom. Sauté until fragrant.
   - Add sliced onions and sauté until golden brown.
   - Add ginger-garlic paste and green chillies. Sauté until the raw smell disappears.
3. Cooking the Vegetables:
   - Add chopped tomatoes, turmeric powder, red chilli powder, and salt. Cook until the tomatoes turn mushy.
   - Add the mixed vegetables and sauté for a minute.
4. Cooking the Biryani:
   - Add the soaked barnyard millet and mix well.
   - Sprinkle biryani masala powder and mix again.
   - Pour 2 cups of water and stir well.
   - Close the pressure cooker lid and cook for 2 whistles on medium flame.
5. Final Touches:
   - Allow the pressure to release naturally.
   - Open the lid and fluff the biryani with a fork.
   - Garnish with fresh coriander and mint leaves.

Serving Suggestions: Serve hot with raita, pickle, or a side salad.

Recipe 46 – Thinai (Foxtail Millet) Tomato Bath

A flavourful South Indian-style millet rice packed with antioxidants, fibre & taste

Ingredients (Serves 2)

Main:

- Foxtail millet (Thinai) – ½ cup
- Water – 1½ cups
- Ripe tomatoes – 3 medium (finely chopped or pureed)
- Onion – 1 small (thinly sliced)
- Green chilli – 1 (slit)
- Ginger – 1 tsp (grated)
- Turmeric powder – ¼ tsp
- Red chilli powder – ½ tsp
- Salt – to taste
- Jaggery – ½ tsp (optional – balances acidity)

Tempering:

- Cold-pressed groundnut oil / Ghee – 1 tbsp
- Mustard seeds – ½ tsp
- Urad dal – ½ tsp
- Chana dal – 1 tsp
- Curry leaves – 6–8
- Hing – a pinch
- Cashews – 5 (optional)

Step-by-Step Preparation

1. Cook the Millet
    - Rinse foxtail millet thoroughly.
    - Pressure cook with 1½ cups water and a pinch of salt for 2 whistles OR cook open-pot style until soft and fluffy.
    - Fluff and keep aside.

2. Make Tomato Base
   - Heat oil or ghee in a pan.
   - Add mustard seeds, let them splutter.
   - Add urad dal, chana dal, curry leaves, cashews, and hing.
   - Add onions, sauté till light golden.
   - Add ginger, green chilli, and chopped tomatoes.
   - Cook until tomatoes soften and oil separates (8–10 mins).
   - Add turmeric, red chilli powder, salt, and jaggery. Cook for 2 more minutes.
3. Mix Millet
   - Add the cooked millet to the tomato mixture.
   - Mix well and cook covered for 3–4 minutes on low heat so flavours meld.
   - Switch off and let rest for 5 minutes.

🍽 *Serving Suggestions*

- Pair with cucumber raita, roasted groundnut chutney, or fryums.
- Serve warm with a drizzle of ghee for extra richness.

💡 Pari's Super Tips:

- Add grated carrots or finely chopped capsicum for a veggie boost.
- Sprinkle flaxseed or sesame powder on top before serving.
- Tomato is rich in lycopene, which supports hormonal and skin health.

Recipe 47 – Kodo Millet Salad with Roasted Vegetables

Pre-cooked / Overnight preparation 😊

Refreshing and Nutrient-Dense Lunch Option

This Millet Salad with Roasted Vegetables is a delightful mix of textures and flavours. It combines the nutty taste of Kodo Millet with roasted vegetables and a zesty lemon vinaigrette. It's light, refreshing, and packed with vitamins, making it perfect for a midday energy boost.

The best part? **It can be prepared in advance and stored in the refrigerator**, making it an excellent choice for meal prepping and packed lunches.

Ingredients:

For the Salad:

- Kodo Millet: 1 cup (washed and soaked for 30 minutes)
- Water: 2 cups
- Salt: To taste
- Roasted Vegetables:
- Cherry Tomatoes: 1 cup (halved)
- Zucchini: 1 (cubed)
- Bell Peppers: 1 cup (sliced)
- Baby Corn: 1 cup (cut into halves)
- Olive Oil: 2 tablespoons
- Salt and Pepper: To taste
- Mixed Herbs (Oregano, Basil): 1 teaspoon

For the Dressing:

- Olive Oil: 2 tablespoons
- Lemon Juice: 2 tablespoons
- Honey: 1 teaspoon
- Salt and Pepper: To taste Fresh Mint Leaves: For garnish

Method:

1. Cooking the Kodo Millet:
   - In a pot, add soaked Kodo Millet, water, and salt.
   - Cook until the millet is soft and fluffy.
   - Allow it to cool to room temperature.
2. Sautee the vegetables you want to use – Onions, bell peppers, carrots, zucchini, snow peas, mushrooms, etc.
3. Preparing the Dressing:
   - In a bowl, whisk together olive oil, lemon juice, honey, salt, and pepSuper per.
4. Assembling the Salad:
   - In a large bowl, combine the cooked Kodo Millet and roasted vegetables.
   - Pour the dressing over the salad and mix gently.
   - Garnish with fresh mint leaves for a refreshing twist.
5. Serving Suggestions:
   - Serve chilled or at room temperature.
   - Perfect for a light lunch or a side dish.

Pari's Super Tip:

- For Extra Crunch: Add roasted nuts or seeds.
- For Added Protein: Mix in grilled chicken, paneer, or tofu.

Health Benefits:

- High Fibre and Low Calorie: Ideal for Pari's Tip.
- Rich in Antioxidants: Boosts immunity and detoxifies the body.
- Diabetic-Friendly: Low glycaemic index helps in blood sugar control.

Did You Know?

Kodo Millet is known as "Varagu" in South India and is traditionally used in temple offerings. It is rich in antioxidants and is known for its anti-inflammatory properties.

Recipe 48 – Browntop Millet Paneer Pulao

Flavourful and Nutritious One-Pot Meal

Millet Paneer Pulao is a delicious and wholesome one-pot meal that combines the goodness of Browntop Millet with protein-rich paneer and aromatic spices. This pulao is a perfect lunch option for busy days when you need a quick, nutritious, and satisfying meal. It's flavourful, colourful, and easy to pack for work or school.

Browntop Millet is known for its high fibre and mineral content, making it a great choice for heart health and digestion. When combined with the protein of paneer and the vibrant flavours of vegetables and spices, it becomes a balanced and nutritious meal.

Ingredients:

For the Pulao:

- Browntop Millet: 1 cup (washed and soaked for 30 minutes)
- Paneer: 200 grams (cubed and lightly sautéed)
- Mixed Vegetables: 1 cup (carrots, peas, bell peppers, and beans)
- Onion: 1 (thinly sliced)
- Tomato: 1 (chopped)
- Green Chillies: 2 (slit lengthwise)
- Ginger-Garlic Paste: 1 teaspoon
- Bay Leaf: 1
- Cinnamon Stick: 1 small piece
- Cloves: 3
- Cardamom: 2
- Turmeric Powder: 1/2 teaspoon
- Red Chilli Powder: 1 teaspoon (adjust to taste)
- Garam Masala Powder: 1 teaspoon
- Salt: To taste
- Ghee or Oil: 2 tablespoons

- Water: 2 cups
- Fresh Coriander Leaves: For garnish
- Lemon Juice: A few drops for extra flavour

Method:

1. Preparation:
   - Wash and soak the browntop millet for 30 minutes. Drain and set aside.
   - Lightly sauté the paneer cubes in a teaspoon of ghee until golden brown.

   Set aside.
2. Tempering and Sautéing:
   - Heat ghee or oil in a pressure cooker.
   - Add bay leaf, cinnamon stick, cloves, and cardamom. Sauté until fragrant.
   - Add sliced onions and sauté until golden brown.
   - Add ginger-garlic paste and green chillies. Sauté until the raw smell disappears.
3. Cooking the Vegetables:
   - Add chopped tomatoes, turmeric powder, red chilli powder, and salt. Cook until the tomatoes turn mushy.
   - Add the mixed vegetables and sauté for a minute.
4. Cooking the Pulao:
   - Add the soaked browntop millet and mix well.
   - Sprinkle garam masala powder and mix again.
   - Pour 2 cups of water and stir well.
   - Close the pressure cooker lid and cook for 2 whistles on medium flame.
5. Final Touches:
   - Allow the pressure to release naturally.
   - Open the lid and fluff the pulao with a fork.
   - Mix in the sautéed paneer cubes.

- Garnish with fresh coriander leaves and a few drops of lemon juice for extra flavour.

6. Serving Suggestions:
   - Serve hot with raita, pickle, or a side salad.
   - Pair it with papad for a complete meal.

Pari's Tip:

- For a Spicier Version: Add more green chillies or adjust the red chilli powder.
- For Extra Flavour: Add a pinch of saffron soaked in warm milk for a royal touch.

Did You Know?

Browntop Millet is one of the rarest and most nutritious millets, known for its high fibre content and detoxifying properties. It is gluten-free and ideal for people with digestive issues.

"Let food be thy medicine and medicine be thy food." – Hippocrates

Conclusion: Power-Packed Lunches/Dinners for a Balanced Life

Lunch is an important meal of the day, and with these millet-based recipes, you can enjoy wholesome, balanced meals that are both nutritious and delicious. Millets are the perfect base for power-packed lunches because they are high in fibre, protein, vitamins, and minerals. They provide sustained energy, improve digestion, and keep you full longer, making them ideal for busy days.

These recipes showcase the versatility of millets – from comforting one-pot meals like Millet Khichdi and Paneer Pulao to refreshing, light options like the Millet Buddha Bowl and Millet Salad with Roasted Vegetables. They are easy to make, quick to pack, and suitable for all age groups.

The best part? You don't have to compromise on taste or convenience. These millet lunch recipes are designed to fit seamlessly into your busy lifestyle, ensuring that you never skip a nutritious meal again.

"Good food is good mood."

I hope this chapter inspires you to experiment with millets in your daily lunch routine. With a little creativity and the right combination of flavours, millets can transform your lunch experience into a delightful and nutritious affair.

So go ahead, give these recipes a try, and feel the difference in your energy levels and overall health.

Let's continue this millet journey in the next chapter where we explore Gut Health and Digestion with recipes that promote digestive wellness and overall well-being.

Happy Cooking and Healthy Eating!

Chapter 11

MILLET SNACKS

"You don't have to eat less, you just have to eat right."

Snacking often gets a bad rap for being unhealthy, but millets are here to change that story. Why reach for nutrient-empty junk food when you can munch on something crunchy, delicious, and good for you at the same time? Before we get into specific recipes, let's chat about why millets make excellent choices for healthy snacking:

- Rich in Nutrients: Millets are packed with vitamins and minerals. A small handful of a millet snack can provide iron, magnesium, B-vitamins, and more – a true power-up for your day.
- High in Fiber: Ever notice how some snacks leave you hungry an hour later? Millets won't do that. Their high fiber content means they digest slowly, keeping you full and satisfied longer. Fewer mid-afternoon hunger pangs mean less temptation to grab unhealthy bites.
- Low Glycemic Index: Millets release sugar into the bloodstream more gradually than refined grains. This is great for sustained energy and even blood sugar levels. In mom terms, that means millets can help avoid those sugar rushes (and crashes!) in your kids after snack time.
- Gluten-Free and Easy to Digest: All common millets are naturally gluten-free. If someone in the family has gluten sensitivity or you're simply looking to cut back on refined wheat, millets are a friendly alternative. They're gentle on the tummy and excellent for all ages – from toddlers to grandparents.
- Versatile & Fun: Millets are incredibly adaptable. You can puff them, grind them into flour, ferment them for batters, or cook them like rice. This means endless possibilities – everything from crispy snacks to hearty side dishes. As you'll see, whether you crave something traditional or a trendy treat, millets have you covered.

In short: Millets bring nutrition, sustained energy, and variety to snacking. As a super-mom (or super-dad, or anyone!) looking to provide healthy options, millet snacks are like little nuggets of goodness you can feel proud to serve.

Now, let's explore some exciting recipes and ideas, starting with beloved traditional bites and moving to modern twists that reinvent millet for the contemporary kitchen.

Get ready – your snack game is about to level up!

Traditional Millet Snacks: Heritage on a Plate

Every culture that grew millets has created its own special snacks and small bites with them. Long before packaged chips and cookies existed, our grandmothers were whipping up millet treats to satisfy those afternoon cravings. By reintroducing these traditional snacks into our routine, we're not only embracing healthier choices but also reconnecting with a heritage of wholesome cooking.

Crunchy, hearty, and time-tested, these snacks have lasted generations for good reason!

Take a trip to a South Indian village fair, and you'll likely encounter ragi murukku, also known as finger millet chakli – beautiful spiral-shaped crackers that are traditionally deep-fried to a golden brown. Made from ragi (finger millet) flour and spices, murukku has a satisfying crunch and a nutty flavor. It's the kind of snack grandma would make during festivals, and kids would sneak a few extra from the jar. Typically fried, we now often bake or air-fry them (more on that soon!) for a guilt-free version that's just as delightful.

Travel west to Rajasthan and Gujarat, and you'll find bajra (pearl millet) being used in snacks like khakra and mathri.

Bajra Khakra are thin, crispy flatbreads cooked on a griddle until they turn into cracker-like snacks. They come in handy as an anytime nibble or as a crunchy side to your evening tea. Spiced with ajwain (carom seeds) or fenugreek, bajra khakras pack robustness in every bite and can stay fresh in an airtight box for weeks – perfect for busy moms who like to batch-prep snacks.

And let's not forget sweet treats! Millets shine there too.

Ragi laddoo (or nachni laddu) is a traditional sweet snack ball made with roasted finger millet flour, ghee, and jaggery, often studded with nuts. These little round delights are powerhouses of calcium and iron (thanks to ragi) and are commonly given to growing children and new mothers for strength. One laddoo with a glass of milk can be a fantastic after-school snack that feels like a treat but is actually nourishing.

Our ancestors truly knew how to make the most of these grains!

Doesn't reading about these traditional millet snacks make you nostalgic and hungry?

Modern Millet Snack Ideas: New Twists for a New Generation

While we love our traditional snacks, the fun really begins when we start experimenting. Modern foodies (and busy parents) have discovered that millets can step outside their old roles and shine in contemporary, even international, recipes. The idea here is simple: take popular snacks or side dishes we already adore and give them a millet-powered upgrade. This way, we satisfy our cravings and sneak in the health benefits effortlessly. It's a win-win!

Think about those days when you or the kids crave something different – maybe a cuisine from a far-off country or a trendy café treat.

6 SMART SWAPS that Will Make You a SUPERHERO in your Friends and Family

1. Craving Italian? How about baking a thin-crust millet pizza base using sorghum or pearl millet flour, and topping it with fresh veggies and cheese.

   You get the same comfort of pizza night, but with a more nutritious crust that's high in fiber and minerals.

2. Looking for a movie-night munchie?

   Try millet nacho chips: bake tortillas made from ragi or jowar flour, then cut into triangles. They come out crisp and ready to scoop up some homemade salsa or hummus.

3. Party at home?

   Impress your guests with little millet tacos – yes, tacos! You can prepare mini taco shells using millet flour (as we'll show you in our recipe section) and fill them with spiced veggies or beans.

   It's an East meets-West fusion that's finger-licking good and way healthier than store-bought taco shells.

   Modern moms are also reinventing bakery favorites with millets.

4. Fancy some cookies or muffins?
   Ragi chocolate chip cookies have become a bit of a trend – they offer a deep, earthy flavor from the ragi that pairs beautifully with the sweetness of chocolate. Plus, they're higher in calcium and fiber than regular cookies, so you can indulge a bit more happily.

   For a quick breakfast-on-the-go or a hearty snack, millet banana bread (like our barnyard millet banana loaf) is filling and flavorful. The natural sweetness of ripe bananas means you can dial back the added sugar, and the millet adds a lovely texture to the crumb. Bake it on a Sunday and you have a healthy snack ready for busy weekday mornings or tiffin boxes.

5. And how about those popular crunchy snacks kids beg for?
   Instead of store-bought fried chips, you can make baked millet crackers at home. Using a mix of millet flour, a bit of whole wheat flour, herbs, and a touch of olive oil, you can roll out and bake your own crackers. They come out crispy, and you can flavor them any way your family likes – think cheese-herb, chili-spice, or even a pinch of chaat masala for an Indian twist.

   These crackers double as a wonderful side to soups or a base for healthy canapés (just add a dollop of yogurt dip or a slice of cucumber on top).

6. Let's not forget energy bars and bites – those on-the-go snacks for your busiest days. Millets like foxtail millet or amaranth (rajgira) can be puffed and mixed with nuts and dates to create nutritious energy bars. Imagine a granola bar, but made with millet flakes and bound together with honey or jaggery. It's the kind of mid-morning pick-me-up that will keep you (or the kids) energized without a sugar crash. You can even involve your little ones in making millet Ladoo balls or energy bites by rolling together roasted millet flour, nut butter, and honey. It's a fun kitchen project and a sneaky way to get them excited about healthy eating.

The possibilities are truly endless once you start thinking outside the box.

So, the next time you're reinventing a recipe, ask yourself: "Can I millet-ify this?"

Chances are, you can - the result will be a snack or side that's trendy and nutritious.

Up next, let's talk about SMART Cooking Methods, how to cook these goodies, because making a healthy snack isn't just about ingredients; it's also about the method.

After all, a millet fritter deep-fried beyond recognition is not quite the healthy bite we're aiming for!

Bake or Air-Fry: A Healthy Twist on Cooking Methods

We all know that how we cook our food can make a huge difference in how healthy (or unhealthy) it is. Many traditional snacks are deep-fried – that's why they taste so irresistible! But as much as we love the crunch, we could do without the excess oil. The good news is, with a few tweaks in technique, we can still enjoy our favorite millet snacks with far less oil and guilt.

Say hello to baking and air-frying – your new best friends for healthy snacking.

Imagine making those millet cutlets or pakoras (fritters loaded with millet and veggies) and instead of sliding them into a pool of hot oil, you lay them on a baking sheet or in an air-fryer basket. In 10-15 minutes, you have golden brown, crispy bites that are just as satisfying. The first time you try air-frying ragi and methi pakodas (a yummy fritter made of finger millet flour and fenugreek leaves), you might just do a happy dance – they come out crunchy without being greasy, and the family will never guess they weren't deep-fried. The same goes for jowar chakli: a traditionally deep-fried spiral snack that we mentioned earlier. Using an air-fryer, you can achieve that delightful crunch with a fraction of the oil. Pro tip: brush the chakli lightly with oil before air-frying to get that perfect crisp and colour.

Baking is equally magical. Many millet snacks like crackers, cookies, or even samosas can be baked. For instance, if you're making a millet and vegetable samosa (think of a savory hand pie), try baking it in the oven. The crust still turns flaky, especially if you give it a light coat of oil or ghee, but it absorbs much less oil than deep frying would. The result? You can enjoy a couple of extra samosas without that heavy feeling. Another example: those bajra mathri biscuits we talked about – they can be baked at a low temperature until crispy. It might take a little longer than frying in oil, but the hands-off cooking time lets you go help the kids with homework or catch up on a favorite show while the oven does the work.

If you're new to air-fryers, here's a quick heads-up: temperatures and times might need a bit of experimenting.

A good starting point for most millet snacks is 180°C (350°F) for about 8-12 minutes in the air fryer, shaking or flipping halfway. For baking, it's usually 170-180°C but for a longer time (15-20 minutes or more) depending on the thickness of the item. Keep an eye on the first batch – once you get it right, you can jot down your perfect settings for next time. And remember, it's hard to un-burn a snack, so when in doubt, err on the side of checking sooner.

One thing is for sure: whether you bake or air-fry, you're making a smart choice. You retain the wonderful flavors and textures of your millet snacks, but cut down drastically on the oil. This means fewer calories, less unhealthy fat, and snacks that won't upset your stomach or diet plan. As a bonus, clean-up is often easier and there's no big pot of used oil to deal with. It's the modern, healthy cook's dream.

"Investing time in healthy cooking today is a gift to your family's future."

That's a little mantra I remind myself of when I pull out the air-fryer or preheat the oven for snack prep. Sure, it might be simpler to just fry something quickly, but then I think about the long-term benefits – how these small daily choices add up to better health for me and my loved ones.

And that is so worth it.

With these cooking methods in mind, let's not forget another way millets can enrich our meals – not just as snacks, but as superb side dishes.

Millet Side Dishes: Small Plates with Big Benefits

Snacks aside, millets also love to share the plate with your main meals as side dishes. In fact, incorporating millets into sides is one of the easiest ways to make your everyday meals more wholesome. Instead of a refined carb or a starchy side, a millet-based side dish can bring fiber, nutrients, and unique flavors to the table. Plus, many millet sides are light and easy to digest, making them perfect accompaniments that don't steal the show from your main dish, but definitely make it healthier.

Salads and grain bowls are a great place to start. Tired of the same old rice or pasta salad? Try a millet salad bowl. Cooked and cooled millets (like foxtail or little millet) have a lovely chewy texture that works beautifully in salads. Toss the millet with chopped cucumber, tomatoes, herbs, a squeeze of lemon, and a drizzle of olive oil – and voila, you have a refreshing side dish that can also double up as a light lunch.

Think of it as a millet-based tabbouleh or couscous salad, but completely gluten-free and extra nutritious. Add some crumbled paneer or feta cheese to it, and even the sceptics in the family will be back for seconds!

Another idea: use millet in place of potatoes or rice in your favourite sides.

For example, a comforting bowl of mashed millets with herbs. Cook a soft millet like little millet or barnyard millet until mushy, then mash it with a bit of milk (or coconut milk for a twist), garlic, and herbs. It turns into a creamy, polenta-like side that pairs wonderfully with grilled vegetables or roasted chicken.

How about millet "fried rice" as a side or light meal? Take leftover cooked kodo millet or proso millet, and stir-fry it with veggies, soy sauce (or our healthy substitutes), and spices to create a fried-rice style dish. It hits the same savoury notes but is much higher in fiber than white rice. Serve it alongside your favourite curry or stir-fry, and you've instantly boosted the meal's nutrition.

For lovers of Indian cuisine, millets can modernize some of our usual sides too. Instead of semolina upma, a vegetable millet upma (using semolina-like little millet) makes a satisfying breakfast or side dish for dinner. Similarly, swap rice with millets in curd rice or other seasoned rice dishes to make them lighter. Even something like a simple millet porridge or gruel, traditionally known as kanji or koozh in South India, can be a soothing side—served with a dollop of yogurt or buttermilk and a pickle, it can accompany spicy curries brilliantly (and calm the palate). These sides not only add variety but also ensure that each part of your meal has a touch of healthy grains.

One of my personal favorite millet sides is millet-stuffed vegetables. For instance, hollow out bell peppers or tomatoes and stuff them with a spiced mixture of cooked millets, veggies, and a bit of cheese, then bake until tender.

You get a fancy-looking side dish that's packed with good stuff. It's also a clever way to use leftover cooked millets— just mix with a few seasonings and you've created something entirely new.

As you experiment, you'll find that millets are pretty forgiving and adaptable. They love soaking up flavors from spices, herbs, broths, and sauces, making them team players in almost any side dish. By making millets a regular feature in your sides, you're seamlessly integrating healthier grains into your family's diet. It's not a drastic change at all – just a smart swap that over time makes a big difference.

Bringing It All Together

We've journeyed through the why and how of millet snacks and sides – from traditional treats that carry the wisdom of generations, to modern innovations that show off our creativity, and the healthy cooking techniques that make them even better. By now, I hope you're feeling inspired and empowered to give these ideas a try.

Remember, every small step counts. Swapping out a bag of fried chips for a homemade millet snack, or serving a millet salad alongside dinner, may seem like tiny changes, but they add up to a healthier lifestyle for you and your loved ones.

"Every time you cook something healthy, you become the superhero of your family's story."

So put on your metaphorical cape (and maybe an apron), and get ready to unleash the power of millets in your kitchen.

Recipe 49 – Finger millet/Ragi Murukku (Chakkali)

Crunchy, Savoury Spirals – Baked or Air-Fried for Guilt-Free Snacking

Ragi Murukku, also known as Finger Millet Chakli, is a traditional South Indian snack that is deliciously crunchy and delightfully savoury. Typically deep-fried, this recipe gives it a modern healthy twist by baking or air-frying it to perfection.

Made with ragi (finger millet) flour, rice flour, and a blend of spices, these spirals are high in fibre, calcium, and iron. Perfect for tea-time munching or as a school snack for kids, this version keeps the nostalgia while upgrading the nutrition profile.

Ingredients:

- Ragi (Finger Millet) Flour: 1 cup
- Rice Flour: 1/2 cup (for crispiness)
- Roasted Gram Flour (Pottukadalai Flour): 1/4 cup (optional for extra crunch)
- Cumin Seeds: 1 teaspoon
- Asafoetida (Hing): A pinch
- Sesame Seeds: 1 tablespoon (white or black)
- Red Chilli Powder: 1 teaspoon (adjust to taste)
- Salt: To taste
- Ghee or Butter: 2 tablespoons (softened)
- Water: As needed to make the dough
- Oil Spray: For greasing and baking (or air-frying)

Method:

1. Preparing the Dough:
   - In a mixing bowl, combine ragi flour, rice flour, roasted gram flour, cumin seeds, asafoetida, sesame seeds, red chilli powder, and salt. Mix well.
   - Add softened ghee or butter and rub it into the flour mixture until it resembles coarse crumbs.
   - Gradually add water and knead into a soft, smooth dough.

   The dough should be non-sticky and pliable.

2. Shaping the Murukku:
   - Grease the murukku press (chakli maker) with oil and fill it with the dough.
   - Pipe spirals onto a parchment-lined baking sheet or air-fryer basket. Keep the spirals evenly spaced for uniform cooking.

3. Baking Option:
   - Preheat the oven to 180°C (350°F).
   - Lightly spray the murukku spirals with oil for even browning.
   - Bake for 15–20 minutes or until crisp and golden, flipping halfway through for even cooking.

4. Air-Frying Option:
   - Preheat the air-fryer to 180°C (350°F).
   - Arrange the spirals in a single layer without overcrowding.
   - Air-fry for 10–12 minutes, shaking the basket halfway through.
   - Keep an eye on the last few minutes to avoid over-browning.

5. Cooling and Storing:
   - Once done, allow the murukku to cool completely on a wire rack.
   - Store in an airtight container for up to 2 weeks.

   Serving Suggestions:

   - Serve with hot chai or coffee for a perfect evening snack.

Pari's Tip:

- For Extra Flavour: Add a pinch of ajwain (carom seeds) or roasted cumin powder to the dough.
- For a Spicier Kick: Increase the red chilli powder or add a dash of black pepper.

Health Benefits:

- High in Fibre and Calcium: Supports digestion and bone health.
- Low Glycaemic Index/Gluten free/Nutrient Rich

Recipe 50 – Pearl millet/Bajra Khakra

(Pearl Millet Crispy Flatbread)

Light, Crispy, and Full of Flavour – Perfect for Guilt-Free Snacking

Khakra is a traditional Indian crispy flatbread that is often served as a tea-time snack or a light breakfast. This recipe uses Bajra (Pearl Millet) Flour, which is rich in fibre, protein, and essential minerals. Naturally gluten-free and low on the glycaemic index, Bajra Khakra is a perfect diabetic-friendly snack that satisfies your crunch cravings without any guilt.

In this version, we're baking the khakra to maintain its crispiness while reducing the oil content. Flavoured with ajwain (carom seeds) and a blend of spices, this bajra khakra is light, crunchy, and super easy to make.

Ingredients:

- Bajra (Pearl Millet) Flour: 1 cup
- Whole Wheat Flour: 1/4 cup (optional for binding)
- Ajwain (Carom Seeds): 1 teaspoon
- Cumin Powder: 1 teaspoon
- Turmeric Powder: 1/2 teaspoon
- Red Chilli Powder: 1/2 teaspoon (adjust to taste)
- Salt: To taste
- Ghee or Oil: 1 tablespoon (for kneading)
- Water: As needed to make the dough
- Oil Spray: For greasing and baking

Method:

1. Preparing the Dough:
    - In a mixing bowl, combine bajra flour, whole wheat flour (if using), ajwain, cumin powder, turmeric powder, red chilli powder, and salt. Mix well.
    - Add ghee or oil and rub it into the flour mixture until crumbly.
    - Gradually add water and knead into a firm, smooth dough. Cover and let it rest for 10 minutes.

2. Shaping the Khakra:
   - Divide the dough into small balls.
   - Roll each ball into a thin circle using a rolling pin. Ensure the khakra is as thin as possible for a crispy texture.
   - Prick the rolled khakra with a fork to prevent puffing during baking.
3. Baking the Khakra:
   - Preheat the oven to 180°C (350°F).
   - Place the rolled khakra on a parchment-lined baking sheet.
   - Lightly spray with oil for even browning.
   - Bake for 8–10 minutes on each side or until crisp and golden. Flip halfway through for even cooking.
4. Cooling and Storing:
   - Allow the khakra to cool completely on a wire rack for maximum crunch.
   - Store in an airtight container for up to 2 weeks.

   Serving Suggestions:

   - Serve with yogurt dip, pickle, or hummus for a delicious snack.
   - Pair with a hot cup of chai or coffee for a perfect tea-time treat.

Pari's Tip:

- For Extra Flavour: Add dried fenugreek leaves (kasuri methi) or sesame seeds to the dough.
- For a Cheesy Twist: Sprinkle grated cheese before baking and enjoy a millet cheese crisp!

Health Benefits:

- Low Glycaemic Index: Maintains stable blood sugar levels.
- High in Fibre and Protein: Aids digestion and keeps you full longer.
- Gluten-Free and Nutrient-Dense: Suitable for all age groups.

Recipe 51 - Navane Dry Fruits Laddoo with Dates

Iron-rich, calcium-loaded, gut-friendly & naturally sweet

Ingredients (Makes 10–12 laddoos)

- Foxtail millet (Navane) – ½ cup
- Seedless dates – 15 (soft, chopped)
- Almonds – 2 tbsp
- Cashews – 2 tbsp
- Walnuts – 1 tbsp
- Desiccated coconut – 2 tbsp
- Ghee – 2 tbsp
- Cardamom powder – ½ tsp
- Optional add-ins: Flaxseed powder, sunflower seeds, pumpkin seeds – 1 tsp each

Step-by-Step Preparation

1. Roast the Millet
   - Dry roast navane (foxtail millet) in a pan on medium heat until aromatic and slightly golden.
   - Let it cool, then grind into a coarse flour. Set aside.
2. Dry Roast Nuts
   - In the same pan, dry roast almonds, cashews, and walnuts until light golden.
   - Coarsely chop or pulse in a mixer once cooled.
3. Prepare Date Paste
   - In a pan, heat 1 tbsp ghee.
   - Add chopped dates and sauté for 2–3 minutes until soft.
   - Mash gently with the back of a spoon to form a paste.
4. Mix Everything
   - In a mixing bowl, combine:
   - Millet flour, coconut, nuts, date paste, and cardamom powder.

- Add 1 more tbsp ghee and mix well.
- While warm, shape into small laddoos.

Storage

- Store in an airtight container for up to 7 days (room temp) or 10–12 days (refrigerated).

Pari's Super Tips:

- Add 1 tsp garden cress seeds (aaliv / halim) soaked in warm water for added iron & hormone balance.
- Roll laddoos in coconut flakes or sesame seeds for added calcium.
- Perfect for kids, menstruating women, and anyone needing a quick iron boost.

Navane Laddoo

Recipe 52 – Foxtail Millet/ Navane Cutlets

Crispy on the Outside, Soft and Flavourful Inside – Baked or Air-Fried

Foxtail Millet Cutlets are deliciously crispy on the outside and soft, flavourful on the inside. Packed with the goodness of foxtail millet, vegetables, and aromatic spices, these cutlets are high in fibre, protein, and essential minerals.

This version is baked or air-fried for a healthier twist, keeping all the crunch and taste without the guilt.

Ingredients:

- Foxtail Millet: 1 cup (cooked and cooled)
- Potato: 1 large (boiled and mashed)
- Carrot: 1 (grated)
- Green Peas: 1/4 cup (boiled and mashed)
- Onion: 1 (finely chopped)
- Ginger-Garlic Paste: 1 teaspoon
- Green Chillies: 2 (finely chopped)
- Turmeric Powder: 1/2 teaspoon
- Garam Masala Powder: 1 teaspoon
- Coriander Powder: 1 teaspoon
- Salt: To taste
- Fresh Coriander Leaves: For garnish
- Breadcrumbs or Oats Powder: For coating
- Olive Oil or Ghee: For brushing or air-frying

Method:

1. Preparing the Mixture:
    - In a large bowl, combine cooked foxtail millet, mashed potato, grated carrot, and mashed peas.
    - Add chopped onion, ginger-garlic paste, green chillies, turmeric powder, garam masala powder, coriander powder, and salt.
    - Mix everything well to form a cohesive mixture.
    - Add fresh coriander leaves for extra flavour.

2. Shaping the Cutlets:
   - Grease your hands with a little oil.
   - Take a small portion of the mixture and shape it into round patties or oval cutlets.
   - Roll each cutlet in breadcrumbs or oats powder for a crispy coating.
3. Baking Option:
   - Preheat the oven to 200°C (400°F).
   - Place the cutlets on a parchment-lined baking sheet.
   - Brush lightly with olive oil or ghee.
   - Bake for 20–25 minutes, flipping halfway through, until golden and crispy.
4. Air-Frying Option:
   - Preheat the air-fryer to 180°C (350°F).
   - Arrange the cutlets in a single layer.
   - Air-fry for 12–15 minutes, flipping halfway through, until evenly browned and crispy.
5. Serving Suggestions:
   - Serve hot with mint chutney, ketchup, or yogurt dip.
   - These cutlets also work great as burger patties or in wraps with fresh veggies.

Pari's Tip:

- For Extra Crispiness: Double-coat the cutlets in bread crumbs or oats powder.
- For a Spicier Version: Add more green chillies or a pinch of red chilli powder.

Health Benefits:

- Low Glycaemic Index: Perfect for diabetes management.
- High Fibre and Protein: Keeps you full and aids digestion.
- Gluten-Free and Nutrient-Dense: Suitable for all age groups and dietary needs.

Recipe 53 – Little Millet Tacos

Crunchy Mini Tacos with a Nutritious Millet Twist Who doesn't love tacos? With their crispy shells and flavourful fillings, they're a favourite across all age groups. These Little Millet Tacos are a healthy, gluten-free version that uses millet flour for the shells, making them light, crunchy, and guilt-free.

Little millet is high in dietary fibre, protein, and essential minerals like iron and magnesium. These mini tacos are filled with a colourful, nutritious vegetable and bean mixture, topped with a refreshing yogurt sauce. Perfect for lunchboxes, parties, or a fun family dinner, they bring a global twist with a local millet touch.

Ingredients:

For the Taco Shells:

- Little Millet Flour: 1 cup
- Corn Flour: 1/4 cup (for crispiness)
- Salt: To taste
- Olive Oil: 1 tablespoon
- Water: As needed to make the dough

For the Filling:

- Mixed Vegetables: 1 cup (carrots, bell peppers, corn, and zucchini – finely chopped)
- Black Beans or Chickpeas: 1/2 cup (boiled and slightly mashed)
- Onion: 1 (finely chopped)
- Garlic: 2 cloves (minced)
- Cumin Powder: 1 teaspoon
- Paprika or Red Chilli Powder: 1 teaspoon (adjust to taste)
- Salt and Pepper: To taste
- Olive Oil: 1 tablespoon
- Fresh Coriander Leaves: For garnish

For the Yogurt Sauce:

- Greek Yogurt: 1/2 cup
- Lemon Juice: 1 tablespoon
- Coriander Leaves (finely chopped): 1 tablespoon
- Salt and Pepper: To taste

Method:

1. Preparing the Taco Shells:
    - In a bowl, mix little millet flour, corn flour, salt, and olive oil.
    - Gradually add water and knead into a smooth, pliable dough.
    - Cover and let it rest for 10 minutes.
    - Divide the dough into small balls and roll them out into thin circles (about 4 inches in diameter).
    - Preheat a griddle or non-stick pan on medium heat.
    - Cook each circle for 30 seconds on each side until slightly golden but still flexible.
2. Shaping and Baking the Taco Shells:
    - Preheat the oven to 180°C (350°F).
    - Fold each circle in half over the oven rack bars to create a taco shape.
    - Bake for 10–12 minutes until crispy.
    - Alternatively, air-fry at 180°C (350°F) for 8–10 minutes.
3. Preparing the Filling:
    - Heat olive oil in a pan.
    - Sauté chopped onions and garlic until golden brown.
    - Add mixed vegetables, salt, pepper, cumin powder, and paprika.
    - Stir-fry until the vegetables are tender.
    - Add boiled and mashed beans or chickpeas. Mix well and cook for 2 more minutes.
    - Garnish with fresh coriander leaves.

4. Preparing the Yogurt Sauce:
    - In a bowl, mix Greek yogurt, lemon juice, chopped coriander leaves, salt, and pepper.
    - Whisk until smooth and creamy.
5. Assembling the Tacos:
    - Fill each taco shell with the vegetable-bean mixture.
    - Drizzle with yogurt sauce.
    - Garnish with extra coriander leaves or grated cheese (optional).
6. Serving Suggestions:
    - Serve immediately for a crunchy, fresh bite.
    - Pair with salsa, guacamole, or a side salad for a complete meal.

Pari's Tip:

- For Extra Crunch: Add shredded lettuce or cabbage as a base layer.
- For a Spicier Version: Add chopped jalapenos or a dash of hot sauce.

Health Benefits:

- Low Glycaemic Index: Ideal for diabetes management.
- High Fibre and Protein: Keeps you full and energised.
- Gluten-Free and Nutrient-Rich: Suitable for all age groups and dietary needs.

Did You Know?

Little Millet is known as "Saame" in Kannada and "Samai" in Tamil. It is one of the smallest millets, yet packed with powerful nutrition, and is considered a superfood for its high fibre and mineral content.

Recipe 54 – Barnyard Millet Veggie Fritters

Crispy, Colourful, and Nutrient-Packed – Baked or Air-Fried

Barnyard Millet Veggie Fritters are crispy, flavourful snacks that are loaded with colourful vegetables and nutritious barnyard millet. These fritters are baked or air-fried for a healthier twist, giving you all the crunch without the grease.

Barnyard Millet is rich in dietary fibre, protein, and antioxidants, making it great for digestion and overall health. These fritters are perfect as appetisers, tea-time snacks, or even as patties for millet burgers. They are easy to make, deliciously crispy, and loved by both kids and adults alike.

Ingredients:

- Barnyard Millet: 1 cup (cooked and cooled)
- Mixed Vegetables: 1 cup (grated carrots, zucchini, cabbage, and chopped spinach)
- Onion: 1 (finely chopped)
- Green Chillies: 2 (finely chopped)
- Ginger-Garlic Paste: 1 teaspoon
- Coriander Powder: 1 teaspoon
- Turmeric Powder: 1/2 teaspoon
- Garam Masala Powder: 1 teaspoon
- Salt and Pepper: To taste
- Besan (Gram Flour) or Oats Powder: 1/4 cup (for binding)
- Olive Oil or Ghee: For brushing or air-frying

Method:

1. Preparing the Mixture:
    - In a large bowl, mix cooked barnyard millet, grated vegetables, chopped onions, green chillies, ginger-garlic paste, and all the spices.
    - Add besan or oats powder as a binder and mix well.
    - The mixture should be slightly sticky but firm enough to shape.

2. Shaping the Fritters:
    - Grease your hands with a little oil.
    - Take a small portion of the mixture and shape it into round patties or oval fritters.
3. Baking Option:
    - Preheat the oven to 200°C (400°F).
    - Place the fritters on a parchment-lined baking sheet.
    - Brush lightly with olive oil or ghee.
    - Bake for 20–25 minutes, flipping halfway through, until golden and crispy.
4. Air-Frying Option:
    - Preheat the air-fryer to 180°C (350°F).
    - Arrange the fritters in a single layer.
    - Air-fry for 12–15 minutes, flipping halfway through, until evenly browned and crispy.
5. Serving Suggestions:
    - Serve hot with mint chutney, yogurt dip, or ketchup.
    - Pair with a bowl of soup or salad for a light meal.

Pari's Tip:

- For Extra Crispiness: Double-coat the fritters in oats powder.
- For a Spicier Version: Add more green chillies or a pinch of red chilli powder.

Health Benefits:

- Low Glycaemic Index: Perfect for diabetes management.
- High Fibre and Protein: Keeps you full and aids digestion.
- Gluten-Free and Nutrient-Dense: Suitable for all age groups.

Did You Know?

Barnyard Millet is known as "Sanwa" in Hindi and is traditionally consumed during fasting days in India. It is rich in fibre, protein, and antioxidants, making it a popular choice for Pari's Tip and diabetes control.

Conclusion: Snacking Smart with Millets

Snacking doesn't have to mean giving in to unhealthy temptations. With millets, it's easy to enjoy crunchy, flavourful bites that satisfy cravings and nourish your body.

As we've seen in this chapter, millets are incredibly versatile, offering a variety of textures and tastes – from crispy Ragi Murukku and Bajra Khakra to fun, contemporary twists like Little Millet Tacos and Jowar Masala Puffs.

These millet-based snacks and sides are not just delicious but also nutritionally superior. They are high in dietary fibre, packed with essential minerals, and naturally gluten free, making them perfect for all age groups. Whether you're looking for a tea-time treat, a lunchbox filler, or a party appetiser, these recipes prove that you don't need to compromise on health to enjoy tasty snacks.

Embracing Tradition with a Modern Twist

This chapter beautifully blends the old with the new. By reintroducing traditional favourites like Ragi Murukku and Bajra Khakra with healthier cooking methods (baking and air-frying), we honour the wisdom of our grandmothers while keeping up with today's health trends. And by experimenting with modern creations like Millet Tacos and

Masala Puffs, we prove that millets are not just for traditional meals – they can shine in contemporary, international dishes too.

Incorporating millets into your snacks and sides isn't just about better health; it's also about reviving a rich food heritage. These ancient grains have nourished our ancestors for centuries, and by bringing them back into our kitchens, we celebrate a legacy of mindful, sustainable eating.

"Healthy eating is not about restriction. It's about balance, creativity, and joy."

"Who knew ancient grains could whip up such delicious joy? Millets make baking fun, wholesome, and full of surprises!"

Joy of Baking

Recipe 55 – Ragi Chocolate Chip Cookies  

Rich, crispy, and packed with fibre!

Ingredients:

- Ragi (Finger Millet) Flour – 1 cup
- Whole Wheat Flour – ½ cup
- Butter (softened) – ½ cup
- Jaggery Powder – ½ cup
- Baking Powder – ½ tsp
- Baking Soda – ¼ tsp
- Dark Chocolate Chips – ½ cup
- Milk – 2 tbsp
- Vanilla Extract – 1 tsp

Instructions:

1. Preheat the oven to 170°C (340°F) and line a baking tray with parchment paper.
2. In a bowl, whisk butter and jaggery powder until creamy.
3. Add vanilla extract and mix well.
4. Sift together ragi flour, whole wheat flour, baking powder, and baking soda.
5. Gradually mix the dry ingredients into the wet mixture.
6. Add milk to bind the dough.
7. Fold in chocolate chips.
8. Shape small balls, place them on the tray, and press slightly.
9. Bake for 12–15 minutes or until the edges turn golden brown.
10. Let them cool before serving!

Recipe 56 – Bajra Almond Butter Cookies  

Nutty, crunchy, and gluten-free!

Ingredients:

- Bajra (Pearl Millet) Flour – 1 cup
- Almond Flour – ½ cup
- Coconut Sugar – ½ cup
- Butter (or Ghee) – ¼ cup
- Almond Butter – ¼ cup
- Baking Powder – ½ tsp
- Cinnamon Powder – ½ tsp
- Salt – a pinch
- Milk – 2 tbsp (if needed)

Instructions:

1. Preheat the oven to 180°C (350°F).
2. In a bowl, whisk butter, almond butter, and coconut sugar until smooth.
3. Add baking powder, cinnamon, salt, and mix well.
4. Gradually add bajra flour and almond flour to the mixture.
5. Knead into a soft dough (add milk if required).
6. Roll the dough into small balls and flatten slightly.
7. Arrange on a baking tray and bake for 12–15 minutes.
8. Let them cool before enjoying!

Recipe 57 – Jowar Oatmeal Raisin Cookies

Soft, chewy, and packed with nutrients!

Ingredients:

- Jowar (Sorghum) Flour – 1 cup
- Rolled Oats – ½ cup
- Coconut Sugar – ½ cup
- Coconut Oil – ¼ cup
- Egg – 1 (or 2 tbsp flaxseed powder + 4 tbsp water as vegan substitute)
- Baking Powder – ½ tsp
- Cinnamon Powder – ½ tsp
- Vanilla Extract – 1 tsp
- Raisins – ½ cup
- Nuts (Optional) – ¼ cup

Instructions:

1. Preheat oven to 175°C (350°F) and line a baking tray.
2. In a bowl, whisk coconut oil, sugar, and egg (or flax egg).
3. Add vanilla extract, cinnamon, baking powder, and mix well.
4. Fold in jowar flour and rolled oats.
5. Mix in raisins and nuts.
6. Scoop small portions onto the baking tray.
7. Bake for 12–14 minutes until golden.
8. Let them cool and enjoy chewy, nutritious cookies!

Recipe 58 – Foxtail Millet Coconut Cookies

Crispy, mildly sweet, and coconut-infused!

Ingredients:

- Foxtail Millet Flour – 1 cup
- Desiccated Coconut – ½ cup
- Ghee – ¼ cup
- Jaggery Powder – ½ cup
- Cardamom Powder – ½ tsp
- Baking Soda – ¼ tsp
- Milk – 3 tbsp (as needed)

Instructions:

1. Preheat the oven to 180°C (350°F).
2. Mix ghee and jaggery powder until smooth.
3. Add cardamom, baking soda, and foxtail millet flour.
4. Fold in desiccated coconut and mix well.
5. Add milk little by little until the dough comes together.
6. Roll into small balls, flatten, and place on the baking tray.
7. Bake for 12–15 minutes or until golden brown.
8. Let them cool and enjoy coconutty goodness!

Recipe 59 – Jowar/Bajra/Ragi Soft & Fluffy Millet Buns

A healthy alternative to regular buns—soft, nutritious, and delicious!

Ingredients:

- Millet Flour (Jowar, Bajra, or Ragi) – 1 cup
- Whole Wheat Flour – 1 cup
- Instant Yeast – 1 tsp
- Warm Milk – ½ cup
- Warm Water – ¼ cup
- Sugar or Honey – 1 tbsp
- Salt – ½ tsp
- Butter (softened) or Olive Oil – 2 tbsp
- Egg (optional, for richness) – 1 (or 2 tbsp curd for eggless)
- Sesame Seeds (optional, for topping) – 1 tbsp

Step-by-Step Instructions:

1. Activate the Yeast
   - In a small bowl, mix warm milk, warm water, sugar (or honey), and yeast.
   - Let it sit for 5–10 minutes until it turns frothy. (If it doesn't foam, your yeast may be inactive.)
2. Prepare the Dough
   - In a large bowl, combine millet flour, whole wheat flour, and salt.
   - Add the activated yeast mixture, butter (or oil), and egg (or curd).
   - Mix everything together and knead for 8–10 minutes until you get a smooth dough. (If sticky, add a little more whole wheat flour.)
3. First Rise
   - Cover the dough with a damp cloth and let it rise in a warm place for 1–1.5 hours, until doubled in size.
4. Shaping the Buns
   - Punch down the dough and divide it into equal portions (6–8 pieces).

- Roll each portion into a smooth ball and place them on a greased baking tray, slightly apart.

5. Second Rise
   - Cover the buns and let them rise for another 30–40 minutes.
6. Bake the Buns
   - Preheat the oven to 180°C (350°F).
   - Lightly brush the buns with milk or butter and sprinkle sesame seeds if using.
   - Bake for 18–20 minutes until golden brown.
7. Cooling & Serving
   - Let them cool on a wire rack for 10 minutes before serving.
   - Enjoy your soft and healthy millet buns with butter, jam, or as a burger bun!

Tips for Best Results:

✓ Use Jowar (Sorghum) flour for soft buns, Ragi (Finger Millet) flour for an earthy taste, or Bajra (Pearl Millet) flour for extra fibre.

✓ If you want fluffier buns, use 50% all-purpose flour and 50% millet flour.

✓ Store in an airtight container for 2–3 days, or freeze for longer shelf life.

Recipe 60 – Bajra/Ragi/Jowar/Foxtail Soft & Delicious Millet Cake Recipe 🎂 🌾

A wholesome, fluffy, and healthy cake made with millets—perfect for guilt-free indulgence!

Ingredients:

Dry Ingredients:

- Millet Flour (Jowar/Bajra/Ragi/Foxtail) – 1 cup
- Whole Wheat Flour (or Almond Flour for GF) – ½ cup
- Baking Powder – 1 tsp
- Baking Soda – ½ tsp
- Salt – a pinch

Wet Ingredients:

- Jaggery Powder (or Coconut Sugar) – ½ cup
- Milk (or Almond Milk for Vegan) – ¾ cup
- Oil (Coconut/Olive/Butter) – ¼ cup
- Egg (or 2 tbsp Yogurt/Flaxseed Mix for Vegan) – 1
- Vanilla Extract – 1 tsp
- Lemon Juice or Apple Cider Vinegar – 1 tsp

Optional Add-ins:

- Chopped Nuts (Almonds, Walnuts, Cashews) – ¼ cup
- Dark Chocolate Chips or Cocoa Powder (for a chocolate version) – 2 tbsp
- Grated Carrot or Mashed Banana (for extra softness) – ¼ cup

Step-by-Step Procedure:

1. Prepare the Baking Tin
   - Preheat your oven to 170°C (340°F).
   - Grease a 6-inch cake tin and line it with parchment paper.
2. Mix Dry Ingredients

- In a large bowl, sift together millet flour, whole wheat flour, baking powder, baking soda, and salt.
- Mix well and set aside.

3. Whisk Wet Ingredients
   - In another bowl, whisk jaggery powder, oil, egg (or yogurt), and vanilla extract until smooth.
   - Add milk and lemon juice and mix well.
4. Combine & Fold
   - Gradually add the dry ingredients into the wet mixture.
   - Gently fold (do not overmix) until you get a smooth batter.
   - Add nuts, chocolate chips, or mashed banana if using.
5. Bake the Cake
   - Pour the batter into the prepared cake tin.
   - Bake for 30–35 minutes or until a toothpick inserted in the center comes out clean.
   - Let the cake cool in the tin for 10 minutes, then transfer to a wire rack.
6. Serve & Enjoy!
   - Slice and enjoy as is, or dust with powdered jaggery/cocoa for extra flavour.
   - Store in an airtight container for up to 3 days.

Pro Tips for a Super Soft Cake:

✓ Sift the dry ingredients to ensure an airy texture.

✓ Do not overmix—stir just until combined.

✓ Use room temperature ingredients for even baking.

✓ Replace milk with buttermilk for extra softness.

✓ Add banana, apple purée, or yogurt for natural moisture.

Variations:

- Nutty Delight: Add chopped almonds, walnuts, and cashews.
- Chocolate Millet Cake: Replace 2 tbsp millet flour with cocoa powder.
- Banana Millet Cake: Replace sugar with mashed banana.
- Carrot Millet Cake: Add grated carrots and cinnamon.

Chapter 12

FAQS: YOUR GUIDE TO MILLETS & HEALTHY EATING

"Curiosity is the compass that leads us to our purpose." – *Unknown*

When it comes to nutrition and lifestyle changes, it's natural to have questions.

Here, we've gathered the most frequently asked questions about millets and healthy eating. Whether you're just getting started or looking to deepen your understanding, this section has you covered!

1. What are millets, and why should I eat them?
   Millets are ancient grains, naturally gluten-free, and packed with fibre, protein, vitamins, and minerals like iron, calcium, and magnesium. They:
   - ☑ Help regulate blood sugar & support digestion
   - ☑ Aid in weight management
   - ☑ Are eco-friendly, requiring less water & fewer pesticides
2. Are millets healthier than rice and wheat?

Yes! Millets have a lower glycemic index, meaning they release energy slowly, preventing blood sugar spikes. They are also higher in fibre and nutrients, making them ideal for:

- ✓ Weight management
- ✓ Diabetes control
- ✓ Better digestion & gut health

3. Can I eat millets every day?

   Absolutely! Millets are safe and beneficial for daily consumption. To ensure nutritional balance, rotate different millets throughout the week:

   - ✓ Monday – Ragi
   - ✓ Tuesday – Jowar
   - ✓ Wednesday – Bajra
   - ✓ Thursday – Foxtail Millet ... and so on!

4. Are millets gluten-free?

   Yes! Millets are naturally gluten-free, making them perfect for those with gluten intolerance, celiac disease, or anyone looking to reduce gluten intake. They are a great alternative to wheat in rotis, bread, and snacks.

5. Can diabetics eat millets?

   Yes! Millets have a low glycemic index, meaning they prevent blood sugar spikes. The best millets for diabetes management include:

   - ✓ Foxtail Millet
   - ✓ Little Millet
   - ✓ Barnyard Millet

   Tip: Keep portions in check—one cup of cooked millet per meal is generally recommended.

6. Which millet is best for weight management?
   - ✓ Barnyard Millet & Foxtail Millet – Low in calories, high in fibre
   - ✓ Keeps you full longer, reducing overall calorie intake
   - ✓ Pair with vegetables & lean protein for a balanced, weight-loss-friendly meal
7. How do I cook millets?
   Cooking millets is easy! The basic ratio is 1 cup millet to 2.5 cups water.
   - ✓ Rinse & soak for 6 to 8 hours or if you lack the time at least 30 minutes

     (*optional for better digestion*).
   - ✓ Cook in boiling water, a pressure cooker, or rice cooker until fluffy.
   - ✓ Use in porridges, pulaos, salads, and even desserts!
8. Can children eat millets?
   Yes! Millets are high in calcium, iron, and protein, making them great for kids' growth and development.
   - ✓ Start with Ragi Porridge or Millet Pancakes (easy to digest & kid-friendly!).
   - ✓ Gradually introduce Little Millet & Foxtail Millet.
9. Are millets safe during pregnancy?
   Absolutely! Millets are rich in iron, calcium, and folate, supporting both mother & baby's health.
   - ✓ Ragi is especially good for bone health due to its high calcium content.
   - ✓ Consume in moderation as part of a balanced diet.
10. Can I eat millets for dinner?
    Yes! Millets are light & easy to digest, making them ideal for dinner. Try:
    - ✓ Millet Soups, Khichdi, or Light Stir-Fries
    - ✓ Avoid over-eating as millets are energy-dense.

When Should Millets Be Avoided?

While millets are incredibly nutritious, they may not be suitable for everyone, especially in certain health conditions. Here's when to be cautious or limit millet consumption:

1. Irritable Bowel Syndrome (IBS) & Digestive Sensitivities
    - ✓ Can You Eat Millets?
        - ☑ Yes, but choose wisely & introduce gradually.
        - ☑ Low-FODMAP millets like Foxtail Millet, Little Millet, and Barnyard Millet are gentler on digestion.

    Avoid or limit:

    Bajra (Pearl Millet) & Ragi (Finger Millet) – High fibre and anti-nutrients may trigger bloating, gas, or discomfort.

    Unsoaked or unfermented millets – Harder to digest, leading to gut irritation.

    Safe Way to Consume:

    - ✓ Soak for 6–8 hours or ferment to improve digestibility.
    - ✓ Start with small portions & monitor symptoms.
    - ✓ Opt for light preparations like soups, porridges, or well-cooked khichdi.

2. Thyroid Disorders (Hypothyroidism & Goiter Risk)
    - ✓ Can You Eat Millets?
        - ☑ Yes, but moderation is key (3–4 times a week).
        - ☑ Prefer Foxtail Millet, Little Millet, and Barnyard Millet over Bajra.

    Avoid excessive:

    Bajra (Pearl Millet) – Contains goitrogens, which may interfere with thyroid function.

    Safe Way to Consume:

    - ✓ Soak & cook well to neutralise goitrogens.
    - ✓ Pair with iodine-rich foods (seaweed, dairy, eggs).
    - ✓ Avoid consuming millets daily if you have thyroid issues.

3. Severe Bloating, Gas, or Slow Digestion

✓ Can You Eat Millets?

☑ Yes, but start with smaller amounts.

Avoid:

Eating large portions of millets suddenly—may cause discomfort due to high fibre content.

Poorly cooked or raw millets—harder to digest.

Safe Way to Consume:

✓ Cook thoroughly—prefer soft foods like porridges & soups.

✓ Drink plenty of water to help process fibre.

4. Kidney Disease & High Potassium Levels

✓ Can You Eat Millets?

☑ Yes, but in limited portions and with medical advice.

Why?

Millets are high in potassium & phosphorus, which can strain weakened kidneys.

Some millets may be too rich in protein & minerals, making it harder for the kidneys to process waste.

Safe Way to Consume:

✓ Stick to small portions (½ cup cooked per meal).

✓ Choose low-potassium grains based on medical recommendations.

5. Anemia & Low Iron Absorption

✓ Can You Eat Millets?

☑ Yes, but proper preparation is needed.

Avoid: Eating millets with tea/coffee—inhibits iron absorption.

Unsoaked/unfermented millets—contain phytic acid, which reduces iron availability.

Safe Way to Consume:

✓ Pair with Vitamin C-rich foods (lemon, tomatoes) to enhance iron absorption.

✓ Soak, sprout, or ferment to reduce anti-nutrients.

Why You Should Listen to Your Body When Choosing Food

Your body is the most reliable guide to your health, and science backs this up in multiple ways.

(1) **Hunger and Satiety Signals:** Your body regulates appetite through hormones like ghrelin (hunger) and leptin (fullness), ensuring you eat when needed and stop when satisfied.

(2) **Biofeedback Mechanisms:** Symptoms like fatigue, headaches, or digestive discomfort indicate deficiencies, dehydration, or imbalances, helping you adjust diet, rest, or hydration accordingly.

(3) **Recovery and Performance:** Muscle soreness, joint pain, or low energy levels signal when to rest or modify workouts, preventing injuries and overtraining.

(4) **Stress and Mental Health Cues:** Anxiety, brain fog, or mood swings often reflect nutrient deficiencies, poor sleep, or hormonal shifts, reinforcing the need for self-care.

(5) **Gut Health and Digestion:** Bloating, acid reflux, or irregular bowel movements indicate food intolerances, hydration needs, or the necessity for dietary changes. By paying attention to these natural signals instead of external opinions, you can optimise health, improve well-being, and build a sustainable lifestyle tailored to your unique needs.

Every individual is unique due to a combination of biological, psychological, and environmental factors, making a **"one-size-fits-all"** approach ineffective in most aspects of life, including health, nutrition, fitness, and personal development.

Throughout the book, we have explored various simple ways of enhancing our lifestyle and diet, which will not only benefit us, but will be a foundation of health for our future generations.

As caretakers, ensuring our children's **health** is just as important as focusing on their **studies** because a **healthy child learns, grows, and**

thrives better. Many parents prioritise academic success while overlooking the **foundation of good health**, which directly impacts a child's ability to focus, perform, and succeed.

Let us be Healthy – Let us Transform our world to be Healthy

☑ **Recipe Index: 1 to 60**

1. Ragi Banana Smoothie
2. Jowar Puff
3. Buddha bowl
4. Kodo Millet Fried rice
5. Bajra power bites
6. Jowar & Egg Pancakes
7. Grilled chicken bowl
8. Bajra berry smoothie
9. Little Millet upma
10. Porso Millet Pancake
11. Brown-top Millet stir-fry noodles
12. Foxtail Millet Kichdi
13. Ragi Mudde
14. Ragi Slurry for babies
15. Jowar roti
16. Bhajra Kichdi
17. Foxtail Upma
18. Sugar-free Ragi Muffins
19. Little Millet Payasam
20. Ragi Ambali
21. Little Millet Ganji
22. Pearl Millet Koozh
23. Millet & Methi Kichdi
24. Barnyard Millet Buttermilk
25. Ragi Almond smoothie
26. Harmone – Harmony Smoothie
27. Sprouted ragi & nut Porridge
28. Foxtail Millet Bisibele bath

29. Chinese style Barnyard Millet Stir fried Veggies
30. Crispy Millet Bhelpuri
31. Millet curd rice
32. Foxtail Millet & Nut Energy Balls
33. Pearl Millet Pancakes
34. Bajra – Millet & Peanut Butter Toast
35. Foxtail Millet & Chickpea salad
36. Bajra & Paneer Protein salad
37. Masala Ragi Ganji
38. Millet chicken recovery soup
39. Millet dosa
40. Pearl Millet Upma
41. Finger Millet Pancakes
42. Foxtail Millet Idli
43. Little Millet Porridge
44. Kodo Millet keerai Masiyal rice
45. Barnyard Millet Biryani
46. Foxtail Millet Tomato bath
47. Kodo millet salad with roasted veggies
48. Browntop Paneer Pulao
49. Ragi murukku
50. Bajra Khakra
51. Navane dry fruit Laddu
52. Navane Cutlets
53. Little Millet Tacos
54. Barnyard Millet Veggie fritters
55. Ragi Choco-Chip Cookies
56. Bhajra Almond Butter Cookies
57. Jowar Oatmeal Raisin Cookies
58. Foxtail Millet coconut cookies
59. Fluffy Millet Buns
60. Millet cake recipes

SAMPLE 3-days Diabetic Meal Plan – Diabetes Management Chapter

SAMPLE 7-days Millet Diet – Lifestyle & Meal Prepping Chapter

Conclusion

A GRAIN OF CHANGE, A LIFETIME OF WELLNESS

As you turn this final page, know that this is not the end—it's the beginning of your own revolution. In every recipe, every tip, and every story shared in this book, lies a deeper truth: **change doesn't have to be overwhelming. It can start with just one millet meal a day.** That small shift has the power to ripple through your body, your family, your community—and perhaps, an entire generation. We've rediscovered the wisdom of our ancestors, combined it with modern science, and now the responsibility rests with us. To heal with food. To live with intention. To share this knowledge with love. You don't need perfection. You just need consistency.

Soak the grains. Stir the pot. Serve with care. And remember—

The revolution begins in your kitchen.

Join the Millet Movement

🎙 **Share Your Story** – If this book has inspired a change in your life, tell us! Tag @AlaMirapNutrition on Instagram or send us your transformation story. You may be featured in our next community spotlight.

📲 **Scan & Connect** – Use the QR codes throughout this book to access cooking demos, meal plans, and bonus resources updated regularly.

👨‍👩‍👧‍👦 **Invite Others** – Gift a copy to someone you love. Inspire a friend, a parent, a neighbour. Let's grow this millet-powered movement together.

Because when one person changes their plate, **a whole family changes their future.**

A HEARTFELT THANK YOU

They say the way to a person's heart is through their stomach, and I truly believe that. Food is more than just fuel—it is love, care, and a way to connect with the people we cherish.

When I began this journey of writing my goal was simple: to help transform lives, one meal at a time. I wanted to show that healthy eating doesn't have to be complicated or restrictive. Instead, it can be joyful, delicious, and deeply fulfilling.

This book is incredibly special to me, not just because it brings together 60 millet-based recipes, but because I had the privilege of co-authoring it with my son, Gururaj Jaggesh. Working alongside him has been one of the most rewarding experiences of my life. His passion, insights, and support have made this book even more meaningful, and I am grateful to share this journey with him.

Through these pages, we have poured in our years of experience, our love for mindful cating, and our belief in the power of small, sustainable changes. Every dish in this book is an invitation—to nourish yourself and your loved ones in a way that is both simple and deeply satisfying.

Thank you for allowing us into your kitchen, for trusting us with your meals, and for taking this step towards a healthier, happier you. We hope these recipes bring you comfort, joy, and lasting wellness, just as they have for our family.

Because in the end, it's not just about the food—it's about the love we serve with it. ♡

With warmth and gratitude,

Parimala Jaggesh & Gururaj Jaggesh

ABOUT THE AUTHOR – PARIMALA JAGGESH

Parimala Jaggesh's journey is a testament to the power of resilience, vision, and the unwavering desire to make a difference. At an age when many settle into the routine of life, she chose to reinvent herself. At **49**, she embarked on a mission—to transform lives through **AlaMirap Nutrition**, a health-tech startup that embodies her lifelong passion for **helping others live healthier, happier lives**.

Her story is not just about **entrepreneurship**; it is about **courage**. Diagnosed with **type-2 diabetes** in 1994, Parimala refused to let her condition dictate her life. Instead, she dedicated years to researching nutrition, blending ancient wisdom with modern science. What began as a personal struggle soon turned into a **purpose-driven mission**—to help people heal naturally, without fad diets or extreme restrictions.

From a young age, Parimala was drawn to **nurturing and empowering** those around her. She believed that true success lies not in personal achievements, but in how much we uplift others. It was this belief that led her to name her company **AlaMirap**—a beautiful play on her own name in reverse. Because for her, the journey has never been about self-promotion, but about **giving back to the world**.

Her work is deeply rooted in **family values**—the warmth of home-cooked meals, the importance of shared traditions, and the strength of a woman who stands as the pillar of her household. She believes that **health starts at home**, and when women take charge of their well-being, they empower their families, their communities, and ultimately, the world.

Today, **AlaMirap Nutrition** is more than just a business; it's a movement. It's a call to women to **prioritise themselves**, to take ownership of their health, and to realise that it's never too late to start over. Through her work, Parimala is proving that no dream is too big, no challenge too great, and no woman too old to change her story.

It's not about the number of friends we have, but about those few who truly **see us—not just as we are, but as we can be**. The ones who believe in us even when we doubt ourselves, who remind us of our strength when we feel lost, and who stand beside us through every high and low. To those precious souls who have been my quiet pillars of support, who have **lifted me, encouraged me, and seen possibilities in me beyond what I could see myself**—this journey is just as much yours as it is mine. **This is my tribute to you.**

To every woman reading this—your journey is just beginning

THE STRENGTH OF FAMILY: MY HEART, MY HOME

For me, family has always been my greatest blessing—the foundation upon which I have built my dreams. I have always believed that true happiness comes from **sharing, growing, and creating together**. No achievement feels complete unless it is celebrated as a family, and no struggle feels too heavy when you have the unwavering support of your loved ones.

I was married in **1984**, to **Mr. Jaggesh**, an actor since 1980s and at present Rajya Sabha Member, and from the very beginning, my husband made me a promise—**that he would always encourage me to study and grow**. It was a promise he kept, a promise that shaped my journey, allowing me to continue learning, evolving, and eventually turning my passion into a mission. His faith in me gave me the courage to **pursue knowledge, build a career, and impact lives** through **Alamirap Nutrition**.

But what makes this journey truly special is that I have never walked it alone. My **elder son, Gururaj**, has been by my side, not just as a supporter but as a collaborator. **Co-authoring this book with him has been one of the most fulfilling experiences of my life.** To work alongside my son, blending my wisdom with his creativity, has been a privilege that words cannot fully express.

My **younger son, Yathiraj**, has been a pillar of encouragement in everything I do. His consistent encouragement and confidence in my abilities demonstrate that passion is boundless, and age is not a limitation. He has always pushed me to dream bigger, to step out of my comfort zone, and to believe in the impact I can create. His unwavering support fuels my journey, making me stronger with every step.

"In a world where such bonds are rare, I'm deeply grateful for my **daughter-in-law Katie** whose support I deeply value in this journey of life."

My little Arjun is not just my **grandson** — he's the sunshine in my day, the calm in my storm, and a reminder that love can be pure, playful, and profoundly healing."

Everything I have built, everything I have achieved, is a reflection of the **love, faith, and strength that my family has given me**. This book is not just about food—it is about the power of **togetherness, the joy of nurturing, and the magic of bonds**.

To every woman reading this—**your relationships are your greatest strength, your dreams are worth chasing, and you are capable of far more than you can imagine. May your life be filled with love, purpose, and the courage to create your own milestones.**

Left to Right – Katie, Guru Raj, Arjun, Parimala, Jaggesh, Yathiraj

"Never in my wildest dreams did I imagine receiving an honorary doctorate—standing there with my family and grandson beside me, I felt the grace of life, love, and unseen blessings guiding every step of my journey."

"In that moment on stage in Paris, I silently thanked God—for making me a diabetic back in 1994. What once felt like a curse became the beginning of a journey to heal myself... and today, to help the world. My peer-reviewed study on food and health was published in international journals, leading me to speak at the esteemed Scientology Conference. And as I stood there, I began with folded hands—'Namaskara, I am from Bengaluru.' Sometimes, our greatest challenges become the doorway to our deepest purpose."

"We started with nothing. Ours was a love marriage—beautiful, but born in struggle. In those early days, we faced poverty, uncertainty, and many storms together. But with God's grace and the blessings of well-wishers, we've come a long way. Today, the greatest joy is that we're able to help others through their own hardships. What was once survival... has now become service."

The Millet Revolution is a heartfelt journey written by two generations—a passionate mother, Parimala Jaggesh, and her son, Gururaj Jaggesh—who have come together with a shared mission: to bring ancient wisdom back into modern homes.

Born from personal health battles, real-life success stories, and a deep-rooted belief in the healing power of food, this book is a guide for anyone—young or old—seeking sustainable wellness.

With easy recipes, inspiring stories, and science-backed insights, it speaks to the busy parent, the growing child, the fitness enthusiast, and even the elderly looking for gentle, nourishing meals. It's not just about cooking; it's about creating a healthier future—one millet meal at a time.

www.ingramcontent.com/pod-product-compliance
Ingram Content Group UK Ltd.
Pitfield, Milton Keynes, MK11 3LW, UK
UKHW041857190726
13854UKWH00002B/947

9 798897 446544